THE INCREDIBLE INTERNET

THE INCREDIBLE INTERNET

<MICHAEL COX>

Illustrated by
Clive Goddard

Scholastic Children's Books,
Euston House, 24 Eversholt Street,
London NW1 1DB, UK
a division of Scholastic Ltd
London ~ New York ~ Toronto ~ Sydney ~ Auckland
Mexico City ~ New Delhi ~ Hong Kong

First published by Scholastic Ltd, 2002
Text copyright © Michael Cox, 2002
Illustrations copyright © Clive Goddard, 2002

10 digit ISBN 0 439 99215 X
13 digit ISBN 978 0439 99215 2

INTRODUCTION
What is the Incredible Internet?

Yes ... the Incredible Internet's all sorts of things to all sorts of people. It's a room full of pals! A ginormous magic cupboard full of astonishing information and exciting experiences which are all available at the click of a mouse.

Well, almost! It's instant excitement! Instant entertainment! And instant knowledge!

The Internet is the fastest-growing communication and information tool ever invented in the history of the world. Billions of emails are sent, and millions of people around the world log on to the Internet every single day! The number of documents posted on the World Wide Web grows by a million a day and is estimated to reach eight billion by 2003 (and that's just the trainer adverts). It's almost as if millions of people around the planet are constantly emptying the contents of their brains, books, newspapers, CD collections and film archives into an enormous treasure chest that anyone can dip into from any place at any time.

In this book you can read about:

- How the World Wide Web was almost called the Mine of Information.
- Which missing bit of his body a man spotted on a website.
- How a gorilla starred in an online chat session.
- How to churn, boink and blog (over 12s only).
- How, in the not too distant future, the Incredible Internet will allow you to experience the smells, sounds, sights and feel of places thousands of kilometres away, all without leaving the comfort of your own cyber-hovel.

And in addition to all that, there are quizzes, guides and stories, a guide to geek speak and a hackers' hall of fame.

OK! Time to boot up and log on...

BEFORE THE INTERNET - TIMELINE

Human beings have been around for millions of years. The Incredible Internet, as we know it today, has only been around for about 20 years or so. But people are already beginning to take it for granted. Just as they used to say...

... we'll soon be saying, "However did we manage without the good old Internet?" So before we begin taking it entirely for granted it might be a good idea to look at what life was like before it existed.

Psssst! Pass it on!

In the time that it takes you to read this sentence a million email messages will have whizzed around the world. It hasn't always been like that! For thousands of years news only travelled as fast as a boat could sail, a horse could gallop, or a man could run (or a small boy riding a giant kangaroo could go

... right the way across the surface of the planet!).

1745 Och aye ... the news! The English whup Bonnie Prince Charlie and his Scots chums at the Battle of Culloden near Inverness. The news takes *eight* whole days to reach London – five by boat and three more by hard riding!

Messages sent across the great oceans are equally slow. A letter sent by sailing ship telling of the birth of a new baby would take months and months and months to reach its destination.

1838 Dot dash dot dot dot.com The electric telegraph is invented in America by Samuel Morse. For the first time in the history of the world, *distance* in communications between humans is suddenly no object! Each letter of the alphabet is represented by a series of dots and dashes and the messages are "tapped out" and sent along wires as electrical

impulses. Instant digital communication has arrived!

1840s Going at a right clip! New, faster "clipper ships" are introduced and journey times are "clipped" by half! So a ship travelling from Hong Kong to New York now takes an amazing *three months* instead of the previous six months.

1876   smokenet.com Several tribes of Native American Indians knock the stuffing out of General Custer and his troops at the Battle of the Little Bighorn. News of the defeat takes *eight* days to get to Mrs Custer who is waiting anxiously back at the fort. However, it's reported that other (somewhat less stroppy) Indians who are mooching around the same fort have been walking around with grins on their faces for days. How?

12

1876 Give us an ... Alexander Graham sometime! Just around the time the Native American Indians are whupping old Longhair Custer, Alexander Graham Bell (1847–1922) invents the telephone and makes the first ever phone call to his assistant (who just happens to be in the next room).

1901 Telephone pioneer Guglielmo Marconi (1874–1937) begins sending the first radio messages across the Atlantic.

1939 On 30 April the first regularly scheduled TV broadcasts are made in the USA. TV broadcasting continued until the start of World War II.

It began again in 1946 after the war.

1956 A stonking great telephone cable is laid under the Atlantic Ocean. It links America with Britain.

13

1965 The first communications satellite is sent up into space. It can relay 240 telephone calls, all at the same time.

1957 American military bigwigs and techno-boffins with brains the size of Brazil get worried about their computer-controlled weapons system and get together to think up a way of outwitting the pesky Russians. The seeds of the Incredible Internet are about to be sown!

HOW THE INCREDIBLE INTERNET CAME TO BE INVENTED - Part One

In the beginning there was ... "The knowledge"!

Unlike some inventions and discoveries, such as disposable nappies, sandwiches and velcro, which were each the ideas of individual inventors, and happened almost overnight, the Incredible Internet was created by lots of people doing lots of thinking, experimenting and chinwagging over a long period of time.

Get set ... net!

Right back in the dim and distant mists of time in the days when men mistook their own heads for coconuts (i.e. about 50,000 years ago), human knowledge was *very* limited (relatively speaking, that is). All the knowledge that the average Stone Age nitwit possessed could probably have been written on the back of a small ~~envelope~~ antelope.

However, things didn't carry on like this for long because people all over the place had lots of *experiences* from which they *learned* stuff and soon the sum total of human knowledge began to grow and grow!

And then, just around the time that there was getting to be so much of this knowledge stuff that it was becoming impossible to remember it all, newfangled talking and newfangled painting got mixed up and produced the even *newer*-fangled writing (around about 3000 BC), which turned out to be a really neat way of storing information.

And so it continued, with people getting to know a lot here and a bit there and a whole lot everywhere, then even cleverer people writing stuff down and storing it in technological miracles known as books (which had been invented sometime around AD 100). Then, because all the sticky-beak scholars and super-brainy scribes in these ancient (and not quite so ancient) civilizations were discovering more and exciting things about the world around them and scribbling all this stuff down on clay tablets and papyrus scrolls and in books the size of suitcases, it became necessary to create somewhere to store all this data. So the newfangled warehouses-of-wisdom known as libraries were invented.

So, the centuries rolled by, the scribes scribbled, the writers wrote and, page by page, volume by volume, the stupendous store of human knowledge grew and grew. And then, between the eighteenth and twentieth centuries, as a result of all the brainstorming, writing, chinwagging, and tremendous technical progress that was now going on all over the place, there was an enormous "EXPLOSION!" of knowledge.

Quite soon there was so much information floating around that awesome alphabetical knowledge catalogues known as encyclopaedias were created as a way of giving people reasonably easy reference to it all. Meanwhile, in towns and cities all over the place, lots more libraries were built to store the ever-growing treasure-trove of fascinating facts, awesome ideas and stunning statistics that were now being discovered as each minute ticked by.

This "knowledge explosion" continued at such a pace that by the early 1900s it became almost impossible to become a "top-of-the-swots-know-it-all" in more than just a few *specialized* areas of knowledge. e.g. **1.** higher mathematics **2.** astronomy **3.** growing novelty moustaches for pleasure and profit. To go beyond that would have required very extreme measures indeed.

It soon began to look as though the ever-expanding store of knowledge built up by humans over thousands of years would become completely unmanageable and almost inaccessible and therefore more or less useless to anyone other than specialists. Suddenly there were millions of books, pamphlets, newspaper articles and whatnot all over the place. And despite the fact that people tried to organize all these acres and acres of information using clever stuff such as library card-indexing systems, it soon began to look like the task of following the thread of an idea through the massive great maze of available data would become almost impossible.

However, human beings are intelligent, inquisitive and resourceful animals who love a challenge (not to mention a Bourbon biscuit and cup of lukewarm tea), so quite soon various brainy bods were putting their minds to the question of how all these vast supplies of exciting knowledge stuff could be stored, retrieved and effectively used for the benefit of the whole human race. One of them is our first...

Cyberspace superstar:
Vannevar Bush (1890–1974)

Despite sounding like something that you would find growing next to your front door, Vannevar Bush was a mathematician, scientist and all round quick-wit. He was also what people call a *visionary* (yes, even without those specs!). This means he had tons of bright ideas about the future and about how people would be doing their thinking and organizing their lives in years to come. In 1945 he wrote an article called "As We May Think" in which he set down his thoughts about how human beings would use science to improve the way they collected all the

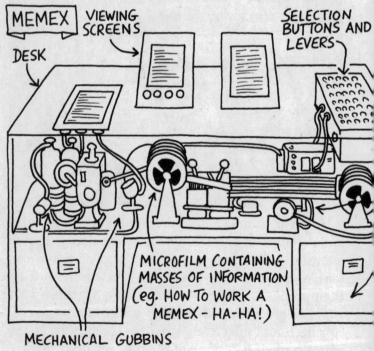

MEMEX VIEWING SCREENS SELECTION BUTTONS AND LEVERS DESK MICROFILM CONTAINING MASSES OF INFORMATION (eg. HOW TO WORK A MEMEX – HA-HA!) MECHANICAL GUBBINS

millions of chunks of information that were now available to them, how they would store the information, and *link* it together to get a better understanding of the world they lived in.

He imagined an information machine which he called a "Memex". He said it would be a desk with viewing screens, a keyboard, selection buttons, levers and that it would have masses of information stored on microfilm[1]. Vannevar didn't actually ever get round to building his Memex machine as it was only his prediction of things to come (and anyway, he was completely useless at DIY). However, if he had done, this is probably what it would have looked like!

DRAWERS FOR
STORING PENS,
BRIGHT IDEAS,
SANDWICHES
etc....

VANNEVAR
BUSH

MORE
MECHANICAL
GUBBINS

[1] Information was stored on microfilm in those days (it still is in a few places). Things like news articles and scientific documents were photographed and reduced until they were microscopically small. This meant that large amounts of data could be stashed for future use. Whenever someone wanted to take a squizz at it they would view it through a magnifying projector. Obviously, Vannevar had no idea that one day microfilm would be replaced by things like magnetic tape, floppy discs and CD Roms. (Come on now, he couldn't predict *everything*!)

Impressive, isn't it? And, remember, the few computers that were around at that time were almost the size of double-decker buses and it was going to be yonks before anyone came up with a computer that had keyboards and monitor screens as we know them today. Vannevar then went on to describe how someone using the Memex would have masses of chunks of information at their fingertips and that they would flit from one chunk to the other, selecting the ones they wanted and putting them side by side to build up a trail or thread of associated *links*, perhaps dobbing in bits of info of their own and occasionally wandering off on side trails.

All this collecting of knowledge from the maze of information that was available to them would eventually enable somebody to build up a big and incredibly useful picture of whatever it was they were studying or researching. Which is more or less how the World Wide Web works today. Except it was going to be another *forty-five* years before someone actually dreamed up the World Wide Web! By which time Vannevar had already logged off from planet earth and flitted up to the great website in the sky.

YES, JUST AS I IMAGINED IT. BUT EVEN BETTER!

It wasn't just the need to find a place to store and access all these oodles of new-found knowledge that would lead to the creation of the Incredible Internet. Around the time Vannevar wrote his visionary "As We May Think" article, the biggest, nastiest war the world had ever known was just coming to an end. Some people were already thinking it would be closely followed by another even bigger, nastier one. And they didn't want to be caught napping!

HOW THE INCREDIBLE INTERNET CAME TO BE INVENTED - Part Two

In the beginning there was also ... FEAR!

Like quite a lot of really useful inventions that have been adapted to peaceful purposes, the Incredible Internet was partly dreamed up by people trying to out-smart and out-clobber other people whom they saw as their enemies (or thought might *become* their enemies).

Back in the 1950s and 1960s, the USA and the USSR (Russia and its allies) were involved in something called the Cold War. This involved glaring at each other from halfway across the world and making threatening noises and gestures, but never actually getting round to lighting the blue touch paper. Which is why it never became a "hot" war. (Phew!) During the Cold War these two "super powers" were also having an "arms race". This is something that human beings have been doing ever since a caveman called Thug noticed that Moron, his Neanderthal next-door neighbour, had a bigger wooden club than him. In other words, the Russians and Americans were both spending tons of dosh on new weapons in a sort of ...

IF THEY'VE GOT ONE OF THEM WE'D BETTER GET AN EVEN BIGGER, FANCIER, FASTER ONE OR THEY'LL HAVE AN ADVANTAGE OVER US AND WE DON'T WANT THAT, DO WE?

... way. Many of these sophisticated and horrendously destructive weapons were controlled by computers. The computers often weren't actually situated anywhere near the weapons but were at command posts where boring-looking men wearing big moustaches and too much aftershave stared at screens all day and picked up telephones and said things like...

RED ALERT! RED ALERT!

YEAH, LARRY. NEXT TIME YOU SEND OUT FOR PIZZAS, TELL MARIO TO GO EASY ON THE RED PEPPERS!

Then one day the American military bigwigs suddenly thought, "Yikes! What if a dirty great Russian nuclear missile lands on our command post? It'll marmalize our main command computer and all the other computers and communications systems and weapons that rely on it! And then we'll be in a right mess. We'd better get the boffins in!"

So in came the boffins (scientists, technologists, men with enormous brains). This is what happened next...

So that was that! A network of equally important computers that could all talk to each other was dreamed up by the men with huge brains. Now, let's have a look at the timeline and see how all these ideas came on in leaps and bounds!

Incredible Internet timeline

1957 The Russians launch their Sputnik satellites into orbit. The Americans are gobsmacked.

They decide to beef up their scientific research programmes and pour tons of dosh into all sorts of projects including defence, space exploration and computer research.

1958 The American government sets up an organization called ARPA. (You don't really want to know what that stands for, do you? You do? OK ... it's Advanced Research Projects Agency. Bet you're *really* glad you asked!) Its job is to come up with all sorts of scientific jiggery-pokery that will put the efforts of the rascally Russians in the shade.

1962 A computer engineer called Paul Baran thinks up an idea which becomes known as "packet switching". It involves breaking digital messages into bite-sized chunks which can be easily sent to other computers. The receiving computers then reassemble the chunks back into messages which can then be read in their entirety.

"Packet switching" is now the way all information is sent around the linked computers, or Internet.

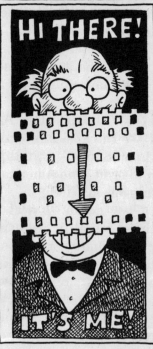

1969 A four *"node"* computer system with high speed links is set up. It's called ARPAnet. (Guess how they thought that name up!) Also, the first ever electronic message is sent between two single computers.

1971 ARPAnet now has *15 nodes*. Scientists and researchers are being allowed to use it too.

The first ever email is sent to a group of computers on the ARPAnet network.

1972 ARPAnet now has *37 nodes*.

1976 The Queen of England sends her first email (and probably thinks it's short for "Elizabeth"-mail).

Early 1980s The military get cheesed off with the scientists because they're actually using the linked computers to exchange ideas ... and to *chat*! (The nerve of it!) The soldiers get all sulky and then set

up their own new network, which they name MILNET – after Mildred, the top General's wife. (No, not really!)

1975 First Altair 8800 "self build" hobby computer goes on sale and causes nerds everywhere to foam at the mouth.

1981 The computer company IBM makes its first ever personal computer.

Mid 1980s The network of linked computers is growing like wildfire. It now has *50,000 nodes*! It links universities and scientific research laboratories. It is becoming known as the Internet.

So, now you know! If *you've* got a computer which is linked into the Incredible Internet, it's not only a PC … it's also a node!

THE WONDROUS WORLD WIDE WEB

So, the Incredible Internet was up and running. But what about the absolutely astonishing invention that many of us now think of as one and the same thing as the Incredible Internet? Yes ... the wonderful World Wide Web itself! Well, just as the wheel had to be invented before the first car could be created and the micro-chip had to be cooked up before the first mini-computer could be made, some incredible inventions needed to be dreamed up before the World Wide Web finally became a reality.

So, while one bunch of boffins were busy developing the Internet, another set of ingenious individuals were hard at work coming up with these three superbly snazzy ideas...

One – Doug's go-anywhere rodent

Around the time the American military bigwigs were getting their bullet-proof knickers in a twist over the threats from foreign super-powers, a cyberspace superstar called Doug Engelbart was trying to  invent a gizmo that would allow computer users to "interact" (i.e. "have a good fiddle with") more easily with the information displayed on their computer screens. This interaction involved moving a cursor (like this: I) around the screen in order to indicate the area where they wanted to fiddle. At this time in the development of computers (1965), the only way

31

the cursor could be moved was by tapping the up and down arrow keys on the keyboard (or furiously headbutting the monitor screen).

These are some of the ideas that Doug came up with in order to make computer users' lives slightly less frustrating:

a) A "light pen" which you lifted and pointed at the screen.

b) A "joystick" (like the ones now used on "zap 'n' splat" PC games). As you waggled the stick, the cursor followed the direction of your waggle.

c) A wooden block with two vertical spinning discs. As with the other devices, however you moved the block, the cursor would mimic the movement on the screen (if you lifted the block and the wheels were still spinning the cursor would continue to move!).

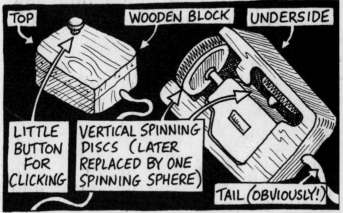

TOP — WOODEN BLOCK — UNDERSIDE

LITTLE BUTTON FOR CLICKING

VERTICAL SPINNING DISCS (LATER REPLACED BY ONE SPINNING SPHERE)

TAIL (OBVIOUSLY!)

d) A gadget which you controlled with your knee. Doug got this idea after seeing how well people controlled the accelerators of their cars by just using their feet and decided that our lower limbs were quite nifty things.

Doug tested all these gadgets by timing how long it took people to move cursors from one point to another and how easy they found it to do. Despite sounding like a good idea, some of the gadgets proved to be quite tiresome when you used them continuously. For example, the testers found that constantly lifting the light pen and touching the screen with it was a right pain in the wrist. (Then again, it did weigh 4,000 billion tonnes – well, nearly.) After the tests he decided that the wooden block had won ... hands down.

Really difficult quiz question (for geniuses only!)

As Doug and his mates worked on the wooden block idea they noticed how the connector cord coming out of its back end made it look like a...

a) Shetland pony
b) fruit flan
c) orang-utan
d) none of these

Answer: d) None of them. Doug and his mates thought that the gadget looked like a *mouse!*

Now, would you Adam and Eve it? Even though almost every one of the world's hundreds of millions of computers has now got its own personal mouse infestation, it was going to be another 20 years before Doug's incredible invention caught on!

Two – Don't get vexed! Get ... hypertext!

Stupid question: How do you read a story? Sensible answer: Unless you're one of those impatient people who immediately turn to the last page to find out who got to snog the gorilla, you start at page 1 and slowly work your way through pages 2, 3, 4, 5, 6 and so on until you come to the end of the book (or fall asleep). This is known as reading in a "linear" or "sequential" way.

However, if you're reading a fact book, or several fact books, to get information you may well dip into one section then flick to another section (possibly in another book) jumping backwards and forwards as your train of thought takes you this way and that.

This is known as reading in a "non-linear" or "non-sequential" way. Unfortunately, reading in a non-sequential way can be a bit of pain, especially if you've got a lot of books to look at.

During the 1960s a man called Nelson (Ted, not Horatio) said it would be really cool if computer technology was used to allow people to read in a non-sequential way, jumping around all over the place, picking up a bit of information here, a few facts there and a ton of knowledge everywhere – much as you do with fact books, but about a zillion times faster and on a much, *much* bigger scale! Which is exactly the sort of thing Vannevar Bush had been getting all excited about when he'd described his imaginary Memex machine 20 years earlier. Ted said that the special sort of writing and publishing that would enable people to do this would be called hypertext. However, a few billion more pages would be thumbed through before the hypertext we all know and click on today would finally arrive.

Three – Ooowee! Ooowee! We've got a Gooey!

About 20 years after Ted had got all hypertext-cited about his non-linear reading idea and Doug had invented his clever cursor-moving device, a couple of technology companies were experimenting with Doug's mouse.

One of the companies was Apple computers who were busy cooking up something called a GUI system. GUI (pronounced Gooey) stands for Graphical User Interface. This was a revolutionary new way of presenting computer contents to the user. The thing is, before 1984, unless you were a scientist, or an incurable nerd (or an averagely intelligent two-year-old), computers were incredibly difficult to use. For starters, if you wanted to tell your computer to do something, you had to type in lots of instructions.

And for finishers, nearly everything associated with computers was presented in "abstract" terms, i.e. heaps of scary numbers and letters, rather than "user-friendly" stuff like simple pictures and easy-to-understand labels. So for complete techno-wimps, for example, writers, publishers, artists, designers and teachers, getting to grips with computers was a right pain in the software. Realizing this, and also realizing that writers and the like are all extremely childish deep down, Steve Jobs and Steve Wozniak, the founders of Apple computers, said…

LET'S PLAY PRETEND! INSTEAD OF HAVING ABSTRACT CODES AND NUMBERS WE'LL HAVE LOTS OF PRETTY PICTURES CALLED **ICONS** THAT THESE CREATIVE TYPES CAN RELATE TO! THE COMPUTER SCREEN CAN LOOK LIKE A REAL "**DESKTOP**" WITH DOCUMENTS AND FILES AND FOLDERS LYING AROUND ON IT, PLUS A DINKY LITTLE WASTEPAPER BASKET (AND MAYBE A HALF-EATEN BACON SANDWICH TOO?) THEN THESE THICK-WITS WILL REALLY FEEL AT HOME!

The lads then incorporated Doug's mouse idea into their Gooey system and...

And it still does! The Apple computers idea proved to be phenomenally fruitful and the creative types all loved it. However, there would always be exceptions...

So that was it! The idea of hypertext had been dreamed up by Ted, and a couple of Apple-cheeked geeks had devised a neat "point-and-click-at-the-icon" system by using Doug's rodent that wasn't a rodent. All it needed now was for someone to come along and put those brilliant ideas together! We'll meet that someone in a couple of paragraphs, but first, this...

For geeks only?

By the time the late 1980s arrived (I wonder what kept them?) the Incredible Internet was growing faster than red hairs on the palms of a mad scientist's hands. Tons of people, like scientists, mad scientists, mathematicians, lecturers and students were finding it incredibly useful for contacting each other and pinging their research findings back and forth.

This is the sort of thing the egg-heads were using the Incredible Internet for during the 1980s. In 1989 a brilliant African mathematician called Philip

Emeagwali did the world's biggest computation. It involved a staggering *3.1 billion calculations* being performed *every single second!* How did he do it? He used the Incredible Internet to link 65,000 separate computers to something called the Connection Machine. Once they were linked, the computers all put their virtual heads together and got stuck into the amazing cyber-sums. When he was asked about his mind-boggling maths project Philip explained he could have used an expensive super computer but that would have been like getting eight oxen to pull a huge wagon. He said that getting all those separate computers involved was more like getting 65,000 chickens to pull the wagon, and that if they were really well co-ordinated chickens they'd make a better job of pulling the wagon than the oxen would.

Professors and swotty students and people like Philip may well have been having a ball with the Incredible Internet but hundreds of millions of ordinary idiots in the street (yes reader, people just like *you*!) were still more or less oblivious to the existence of the scintillating new adventure playground known as cyberspace. But then someone invented the astonishing thing that would change all of that for ever. And that someone is our next...

Cyberspace superstar
Tim Berners-Lee
(1955–)

A lot of people think of Tim as Mr World Wide Web.

He was born in London in 1955 and his mum and dad worked in the computer industry. As a result, tiny Tim often spent his time playing with bits of dead computers and building model computers out of cardboard boxes. After going to school and vastly extending the contents of his in-head database (i.e. learning stuff and whatnot) he went to Oxford University where he studied physics and electronics. When he left Oxford in 1976 he worked on useful things like those bar codes you now see on almost everything you buy, but eventually he went to work at a really famous physics laboratory called CERN (stands for European Centre for Nuclear Research, when it's written in French). CERN was based in Geneva in Switzerland but had masses of researchers working on mountains of different projects at loads of different laboratories ranged all around the world. In order to help himself remember who was doing what, where, and when, and how all the various boffins and tasks were

41

linked, Tim wrote a computer program which he said was "a memory substitute" – in other words, a rather more sophisticated version of lots of little lists scribbled on a scrap of paper all joined up with coloured arrows.

He called the program Enquire-Within-Upon-Everything, after the title of a Victorian reference book he'd enjoyed during his childhood (not that he was a Victorian child or anything).

Tim for a change

Tim's "Enquire" idea remained in his head and a few years later, after having had a break from CERN, he went back to work there again. Not only did CERN have lots more boffins scattered about the globe getting up to all manner of miraculous scientific shenanigans but now they were also all using different computers and software which made the whole matter of effective communication a huge pain in the keyboard. For instance, this sort of thing would cheese Tim off no end:

BUONGIORNO, TIM! ABOUT PROJECT Z. COULD YOU JUST RUN THROUGH YOUR CURRENT DATA AGAIN?

YES, WELL IT INVOLVES A VARIEGATED WIDGET SPRANK UNDERPINNED BY THREE BOFFWOFFLERS AND A SPRENULLATED THROGSCOPE ALONG WITH...

20 MINUTES LATER —

ER, TIM, ABOUT PROJECT Z. COULD YOU JUST RUN THROUGH THE BASICS AGAIN?

YES, WELL IT INVOLVES A VARIEGATED WIDGET SPRANK UNDERPINNED BY THREE...

ANOTHER 20 MINUTES LATER—

GUTENMORGEN, TIM. VOT IZZ ZE GEN ON PROJECT Z?

YES, WELL IT INVOLVES A VARIEGATED WIDGET SPRANK UNDERPINNED BY THREE...

After frustrating episodes like this, Tim thought how much easier it would be for his colleagues to find out what he was up to and for *him* to find out what *they* were up to if they had a nice, simple, straightforward system that enabled them to *share* all of their thousands of documents without any fuss or bother. In other words, something rather like his Enquire program but on a much bigger, *global* scale! So, he got busy working on a computer program that would eventually become the whopping great global information system that we all now know and surf. As Tim himself said, other people like Doug, Ted and the two Steves had already sorted the basics for his great new idea. All he had to do was link them to create the amazing phenomenon known as the...

Cyberbyte
The World Wide, er ... Mesh?

Once Tim had gathered his thoughts on how his new idea would work he began wondering what to call it. Here are some of the names he thought of before he came up with the World Wide Web...

1. The "Information Mesh" or the "Mesh" – Tim didn't like this because it sounded a bit like "mess" (especially if you said it when you were really drunk).

THIS IS ANOTHER FINE OLD MESH YOU'VE GOT USH INTO!

2. "Mine Of Information" – Tim didn't like this either because shortened to an acronym it spelt the word *MOI*, which is French for ME! And, being an extremely modest person, the last thing Tim wanted to sound was big-headed or conceited.

3. "The Information Mine" was the next one he thought of. But then he tried shortening that to an acronym. And as far as TIM was concerned that would have made him seem like even more of a show off!

How Tim wove the World Wide Web

Tim's main idea was to create a single "global information space" in which people from all around the world could share their knowledge, ideas and brainwaves.

And he wanted them to be able to put in or get hold of that information quickly and easily. And he definitely didn't want that information space to be controlled by one person or group of people.

He wanted it to belong to everyone in the world. But before he could make all this happen he had to overcome some problems:

Problem one

The Internet was a disorganized and chaotic place with thousands of techno-bods communicating using lots of different sorts of computers and different computer codes; rather like a marketplace full of people all speaking different languages and using lots of interpreters to understand each other.

Solution Tim's plan was to replace all the different computer languages used on the Internet with just *one* single new computer language! So, basing it on

46

Ted's clever bouncing-from-one-chunk-of-info-to-another "<u>hypertext</u>" idea, he invented a new computer language called HTML (HyperText Mark-up Language).

HTML is the universal language of the Web and is used by people who put text, sound and pictures on web pages. Hypertext is easy to recognize because it usually contains those coloured underlined words that are known as <u>hypertext links</u>.[1] Clicking on them is like bouncing on a springboard that sort of *pings* you to a new (but related) area of information.

[1] Important note to netheads, geeks and nerds. Whilst reading all of this please do not attempt to "*click*" on any of the <u>underlined text</u>. This is a page in a *book*; not a page on a website. Clicking on it will make you look stupid. So will attempting to scroll, highlight or drag text.

Problem two A device was needed to allow the underlined hyper-link words in documents to link instantly to other documents.

Solution Tim wrote a computer program containing a "protocol" (a set of rules) which dictated how information should be transferred from computer to computer on the World Wide Web. He called it HyperText Transfer Protocol (HTTP). It instantly took users straight from an <u>underlined link</u> to a new document. Ping!

Problem three To get to a piece of information that was stored on another computer, people had to type in a long series of instructions. Hard going if you weren't a computer whizz! One mis-typed letter or number and you were up Byte Creek without a paddle.

Solution Tim devised a simple address system that any dimwit (yes, even *you*, reader!) could understand. He called it the URI, which stands for Universal Resource Indicator, but it's now known as the URL which stands for Universal Resource Locator. (Don't ask!) http://www.herdofnerds.info is a really simple example of a web address. The "http" bit tells you that the address is for a web page. The "www." stands for World Wide Web (as if you didn't know!), the "herdofnerds" bit tells you the name of the "host" organization supplying the web pages, while ".info" indicates that it's a document or bunch of documents published by an information organization. Once a document had a URL on it, it could be posted on a specific server and found by a nifty bit of software known as a … well, read the next bit and you'll find out!

Problem four The ordinary chump in the street didn't have anything to look at Tim's wonderful Web with.

Solution Tim created the World Wide Web's first ever *browser* so that users anywhere on the planet could view the contents of his great creation on their computer screens. A browser is a computer software program that

makes it possible for us to find our way around the World Wide Web and take a squizz at the pages contained on it.

Get lost! It's for everyone!

When word eventually went round that Tim had got his World Wide Web software program sorted he was approached by big businessmen who wanted to give him tons of dosh for his great new invention so that they could charge everyone else in the world tons of dosh to use it.

But Tim said "No" because he wanted everyone to have free access to it. Rather than making mountains of money from his brainwave Tim was more interested in the fact that his invention had proved you can have an idea and actually make it happen! He said he wanted it to be an example to all the dreamers in the world to keep plugging away at their own brainwaves and not give up! And that's the way it's stayed.

Wondrous World Wide Web – ~~Tim line~~ timeline

1945 Vannevar Bush dreams of his Memex machine.

1964 Ted Nelson writes about his hypertext idea.

1965 Doug Engelbart makes his mouse.

1980 Tim Berners-Lee writes his "Enquire" program.

1984 Steve Jobs and Steve Wozniak go all Gooey.

1990 Tim gets cracking on his World Wide Web invention and on Christmas Day he and his buddies at CERN turn on their web server (the thingy that sends WWW pages to WWW browsers). It's the first in the world and its address is cern.ch.

1990 An American politician called Al Gore gets all excited about the World Wide Web and calls it the Information Superhighway (and later that same day a virtual hedgehog is squashed flat by some speeding hypertext).

1991 The first ever web browser is made available for the public to buy so that they can do that thing where you keep nipping from one website to another and having a squizz at this 'n' that.

51

1992 A writer dreams up the phrase *"surfing the net"* and at last everyone knows what they're doing.

1993 A 22-year-old whizz-kid called Marc Andreessen writes a web browser program called Mosaic which allows people to see *pictures* on the World Wide Web for the first time. Tim Berners-Lee isn't at all keen on the idea of adding pictures to the Web and is said to have had "words" (but definitely not pictures) with Marc. Mosaic eventually becomes Netscape and, almost overnight, Marc becomes a multi-millionaire.

1994 The Prime Minister of Japan and Pizza Hut go online (not on the same website though). The Web is growing at a rate of 341,634% a year! There are now 10,000 web servers online. It's a nightmare to find your way around all the addresses and different web pages.

Two students have the bright idea of creating something called a search engine to help people "navigate" their way around them all. They call it Yahoo.

1996 There are now 230,000 web servers online. The domain (website) name tv.com is sold for $15,000!

1997 A million websites are online. The domain name business.com is sold for $150,000.

1998 The Incredible Internet is growing by leaps and bounds. More than 102,000,000 people around the world are now using it. However, only 5% of all the people in the UK are online.

1999 A British company called lastminute.com starts flogging last-minute discount holidays and gifts and stuff over the Internet. Six months later, when its shares start selling on the stock market, Martha Lane-Fox, one of its founders, is said to be

"worth" £49 million. Internet fever spreads like a supervirus. Everyone's talking about the World Wide Web. Thousands of people who hope to get rich set up Internet e-commerce companies selling everything from toothpicks to tortoises.

2000 Over six million homes in the United Kingdom are now connected to the Internet. An Internet company called boo.com sets up to sell fashion clothes, spends squillions of pounds, then goes bankrupt (and is quickly renamed boohoo.com).

2001 More than ten million homes in the UK are now connected. A new one goes online for the first time every *eight* seconds (and the man doing the wiring says he's exhausted). Over 500 million people in the world are now online!

2002 544.2 million people are online worldwide, and the numbers are still rising!

Sticky-beak search engines

Search engines use little software robots called spiders or web-crawlers which are constantly wandering around the millions of pages on the World Wide Web, taking a squizz at them, then remembering all the places they've been so that they can build up a humungous great list of everything they've had a butchers at. So, when you bang in your request for, say:

... it goes rushing off to find the sites that best match your (peculiar) tastes then displays them so that you can click on all the hyperlinks and find out more (you weirdo). But that's not all! As thousands and thousands of new pages are added to the World Wide Web each day the spiders rush madly around collecting more and more data about them in an effort to keep pace with the ever-expanding network.

Cyberbyte
Bricks 'n' clicks

Larry Page, the boss of the huge "Google" Internet search engine, once built himself a working inkjet printer out of Lego bricks.

Cybertrivia quiz

One of the following phrases is an anagram of Information Superhighway – you have ten seconds to jiggle the letters to work it out. Or get your computer to do it for you.

a) Hi ho! Yow! I'm surfing the Arpanet!
b) Enormous hairy pig with fan.
c) Waiting for a promise, huh?
d) A rude whimper of insanity.

Answer: b)

56

SPEAK LIKE A GEEK

Nearly all new inventions and ideas are accompanied by a whole new way of speaking. The arrival of the Incredible Internet has created an entire new language which it would take a whole book to describe, translate and understand.

Which, of course, isn't possible, so to be going on with, here's a little taste of...

How to speak geek

Alpha Geek If you're an Alpha Geek you're the bee's knees when it comes to knowing all there is to know about the Internet and computers. However, you may not know all that much about anything else.

Being under "mouse arrest" Having done something which has upset your Internet service providers so much that they've denied you access to the web.

Boinking Meeting up for real with people who you've chatted to over the Internet.

Blogging This is what people who have their own websites do. It comes from the phrase "web log" which means a sort of web diary in which bloggers make a new entry each day for other surfers to read. They chat about what's been going on in the world, what's new on the Internet and other matters that might be of interest.

Churning Reader, people who run websites and service providers and sell techy things lie awake at night worrying that *you* are going to do this. Why? Because churning means losing interest in a product, service or website then wandering away never to return again. In order to stop you churning, the biz whizzes do their best to *motivate* you with exciting things to do and see. They call this making their websites, gizmos and services *sticky*, which more or less means sticky like fly paper. Yes, the last thing they want is for you to buzz off!

Cobweb site A website that's not been updated for some time.

Very frustrating especially if you're doing research ... but at least they all eventually do get thrown away on World Internet Cleaning Day! (See page 123.)

Dead tree edition The paper version of something you can see in electronic form on the net. So is that why they call it *logging* on?

Digerati This is the name given to all the big cheeses in the world of the Internet and computing, for example Bill Gates, Tim Berners-Lee, Steve Wozniak, Steve Jobs.

Dorito syndrome Feeling of emptiness and dissatisfaction you get after doing something that's not necessarily good for you (like eating tons of spicy crisps), as in...

Probably comes from consuming vast quantities of computer spam (see page 62).

Ego-surfing Putting your own name into a search engine on the Internet in the hope that it will come up with at least one website saying you are the most talented, popular, handsome, successful and rich human being who ever walked the planetscape. Something that writers never do...

Flame mail Angry email messages sent by people who are...

Grey bar land Your grey bar's the little doofer that creeps across your screen to indicate progress on loading a site. Grey bar land is the place your brain goes as you wait for this seemingly endless process to finish. Some people seem to spend most of their lives in grey bar land ... even when they're not in front of a computer.

Gronking out What you do when you've surfed yourself silly – i.e. you stop using the Net for a while. (Two minutes?)

Internesia You may have suffered from this yourself. It's the amnesia (memory loss) you experience when you're surfing. You know you've seen a bit of information but you've been to so many sites you can't for the life of you remember which site you saw it on.

Link rot Nothing to do with dodgy sausages! This means the <u>hypertext links</u> on a website are more or less useless.

If the links are duff it probably means the website is pretty hopeless too and that it's more than likely a...

404 Someone (or something) who's thought to be pretty useless. It comes from that message which comes up telling you a site or document you've tried to get to can't be located: **Error 404 URL not found.**

Lurking This is what some people (404s?) do when they visit an Internet chat room (website where people natter to each other via emails). Rather than joining in the conversation they just sort of hang around checking out what everyone else has to say. A bit like hiding in the cupboard at a party...

Netizen A citizen of cyberspace. Netizens frequently use the Incredible Internet for all sorts of things and, just like Tim Berners-Lee, they believe that it's there for everyone to contribute stuff to and take stuff from.

Newbie Someone new to Internet use or a particular area of the Internet.

Open collar workers People who use the Internet to work from home. Called this because they don't have to wear a tie to work. Not always the case though!

Shouting This describes the practice of sending messages in UPPER CASE (CAPITAL LETTERS) to make people aware that you are really, really ... ANGRY!! Possibly about receiving a load of this stuff...

Spam – emails that try to sell you stuff and adverts on websites ... like those annoying pop up ones.

World Wide Wait What some people say WWW really stands for because connections sometimes take so long to happen that it feels like it would have been quicker to have got on your bike and gone round to the house or office of the person whose website you wanted to look at.

THE WORLD WIDE DASH FOR DOT.COM DOSH

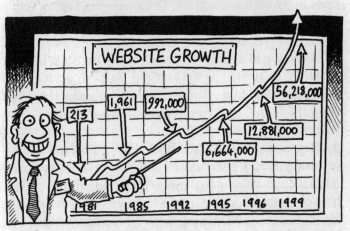

Tim's World Wide Web invention was a phenomenal success! So much so that people began thinking of the Incredible Internet as the World Wide Web. And the World Wide Web as the Incredible Internet! In no time at all hundreds of thousands of individuals and organizations were rushing to set up sites on the wonderful World Wide Web, advertising their businesses on it, telling jokes on it, selling things, visiting chat rooms, doing their studies on it and buying things from it.

And, even though Tim had actually intended it to be a tool for information and education, lots of people began making huge fortunes from it! And because so many Internet businesses end their URL (web address) with the suffix ".com" the newly wealthy Web whizz kids and Internet entrepreneurs became known as "dotcom millionaires"! Even children, like 12-year-old Tom Hadfield, were able to make mountains of money! Fancy making some serious cyberspace spondulicks and becoming a dotcom capitalist yourself? Take some tips from Tom!

Six steps to web wealth

1. Have a pal whose already a bit "web wise" In 1994 12-year-old Tom Hadfield went round to his pal Rupert's house. Rupert had a computer that was connected to the newfangled thingy called the Internet.

2. Get completely hooked When Tom saw it he was so gobsmacked that he didn't go home for three whole days. When his mum and dad finally asked him if he'd mind coming back to his own house (as his dinner was turning green) he said he would, but only if he could have an Internet connection like Rupert's. They agreed, and not long afterwards Tom went online and was soon whizzing off emails to new cyber-buddies all around the world.

3. Have a brill idea One day when he was visiting a cyber chat room, an e-pal in Australia asked if anyone knew the score from the Arsenal match, so Tom typed back:

He began to discover that English soccer fans all over the world were always desperate for footy news but usually had to get it from the UK newspapers which took at least a couple of days to arrive from the UK (British paper boys and girls being such terribly slow swimmers). This gave Tom the idea of sending out match results in emails.

THREE ALL! THEY'VE GONE INTO EXTRA TIME!

4. Get a great name for your site However, this didn't keep Tom's e-mates satisfied and they soon began asking for more info like match reports, referees' names, crowd attendance figures (and ratings out of ten for the hot meat pies). Suddenly, instead of just ten or so people wanting info, it was 200. So Tom thought, "I'll put it all on my own website which I'll call Soccernet!"

5. Expand your site Once the site was up and running Tom added player biographies and all sorts of other interesting stuff and soon thousands of people were visiting it every day.

6. Flog it to the highest bidder Eventually a big newspaper got interested in Tom's site so he and his dad sold it to them for lots of dosh. Not long after that the newspaper sold a huge chunk of it to the Disney Corporation for $25 million (about £16,000,000)! In 2000, Tom's slice of the Soccernet action was said to be worth around $11 million (about £8,000,000) but as he was still a schoolboy and wasn't all that bothered about spending the dosh anyway, he immediately got busy on his next idea. This is the Schoolsnet site which is packed with info for teachers, pupils and parents, and also said to be worth millions. So – what are you waiting for?

Way to go?

Sometimes, being an Internet whizz kid has its drawbacks. When Ben Way was eight he was having tons of problems reading and writing due to his dyslexia so the local council gave him a computer to help him improve his skills. As well as helping him with his school work the PC got him hooked on all things connected with computers. Despite Ben's efforts to improve, a couple of his teachers told him he would never amount to much. Ben decided to prove them wrong and by the time he was 15 he'd set up his own business helping people sort out problems with their computers. Not long after this he had the idea of creating a search engine that would help business people by cutting down the amount of time they spent looking for stuff on the Web. He called his site Waysearch.com and it was so successful that he gave up working for his A-level exams so he could give all his time to it. Some high-powered business bods decided to invest millions of pounds in Ben's idea. However, they didn't just see themselves as buying a slice of Ben's business action. They decided they'd more or less bought a chunk of him too, as his whizz kid image would be really cool for the business. And naturally, the last thing they wanted was for their wonder-boy to be getting into bad ways. Or spending all the dosh and spilling valuable business secrets to rival companies! So, before they handed over their money, Ben had to promise that he wouldn't do any of the following things before his 21st birthday:

1. GET A TATTOO

2. SMOKE

3. DYE HIS HAIR

4. GO OUT AFTER ELEVEN O'CLOCK AT NIGHT UNLESS ACCOMPANIED BY SOMEONE THEY CHOSE TO LOOK AFTER HIM

5. GET DRUNK

6. CHANGE HIS APPEARANCE IN A BIG WAY

Cyberbyte

Tom and Ben are quite ancient compared to some Web whizz kids. In 2001 a four-year-old Indian boy called Ajay Puri gave a demonstration at a computer college during which he showed the staff and students how to design a website. Ajay, who was born in 1996, had been using computers since he was knee-high to a modem (i.e. 18 months). By the time he was four he was able to make fully functioning websites that included hyperlinks, thumb-nail-sized pictures, background music and all the trimmings. He had also mastered a whole heap of other cyber-skills including typing out documents, creating graphs and sorting out data lists.

AREN'T YOU INTERESTED IN TOYS?

OF COURSE I'M INTERESTED IN TOYS! I'VE JUST CREATED A CROSS-INDEXED DATABASE OF ALL OF THEM!

http/www:wots its flippin name.com?

Tom and Ben had catchy names for their sites. If you've got a website and want millions of surfers to come to it the best thing to do is give it an unforgettable name or a name that tells people exactly what it's all about. This title is known as a domain name. When everyone was getting excited about the World Wide Web in the late 1990s, stacks of people realized just how important website names were going to be so they went domain-name crazy and rushed to register thousands and thousands of them so that they could use them or sell them to other people.

Spottybot.com?

Procter and Gamble, the huge company that sells lots of the useful "personal hygiene" stuff you see in the supermarkets, were really quick off the mark in registering domain names. Some of the website names they chose were very direct and to the point and there was definitely no mistaking what they were going to be selling from them. Here are five of the names they registered mixed up with five false ones. See if you can spot the pharmaceutical fakes:

1. badbreath.com
2. itchybum.com
3. dandruff.com
4. really-got-the-runs.com
5. sweatypits.com
6. bottyburps.com
7. pimples.com
8. underarm.com
9. diarrhoea.com
10. niffy-whiffs.com

SOUND LIKE MY KIND OF SITES!

FNURRP!

Answers: 2, 4, 5, 6 and 10 are false. All the rest are true! Those business wizards certainly know how to give their products glamour appeal.

Ewe must be kidding!

Hoping to make a great deal of money quickly, some people tried to register the website names of big businesses before the companies themselves could actually get round to it. These cyber-pirates, as they are known, did this in the hope that they could eventually sell the big companies their own website names. In 2000, one cyber-pirate named his website Baa.com and filled it with lots of information about sheep. Not long afterwards he offered to sell the website to the massive British Airport Authority for two million pounds.

Not everyone rushed to make money out of web addresses. Some people were sitting on a cyberspace fortune and didn't even know it...

Desert island dosh

Most countries have a World Wide Web international code which is tagged on to the end of web addresses. For example, France is fr, Britain is uk and Germany is de. America is the only country which doesn't have one of these codes because that's the place where the Internet kicked off and about half the dot.com companies in the world are based there anyway. The islands of Tuvula in the Pacific have the code tv. However, the people who live on them haven't even got TVs or newspapers, never mind the Incredible Internet, so the only surfing they're likely to do is in the waves of the Pacific Ocean. Realizing that the Internet and TV would soon be merging into one huge all-singing, all-dancing box of tricks, a Californian Internet company decided they'd really like to own tiny Tuvula's "tv" suffix so they could sell it on to all the other world companies who'd like to be called things like www.internet.tv or www.bbc.tv … or whatever. So, what do you think they offered Tuvula for their precious two letters?

EENIE MEENIE...

LOADSA CASH

a) $5

b) $50,000,000

c) $5,000

d) $500

e) some fish

Answer: b) They paid the Tuvulans $50,000,000 for them! That's about 34 million quid! Which works out at around £3,500 for each islander … or, to put it another way, 25 years' worth of wages!

Cyberbyte
An Israeli man called Tomer Krrissi was so dotty about Tim's World Wide Web idea that he officially changed his name to .com! Then again, with a name like his, who can blame him!

They're just wild about Harry

Harry Potter fanatic Claire Field set up her www.harrypotterguide.co.uk website but Warner Brothers, the ginormous entertainment company, weren't too chuffed about this because they own all the film rights to the Harry books and are also entitled to flog tons of Harry Potter merchandise (collars for three-headed dogs, turbo-charged broomsticks, that sort of thing). They sent her a letter asking her to hand over the site name to them. As you'll no doubt agree, they obviously had a point, as it was remarkably unfair and cruel of this lone 15-year-old girl to pick on a helpless multi-billion-dollar entertainment giant like them and try to steal their goodies. However, lots of other Harry Potter fans didn't agree and got all riled up so Warner Brothers eventually said she could keep the site if she made it clear that Harry belonged to them.

Thousands of people have realized that the Incredible Internet is a great place to buy and sell things from. Setting up a website is like opening a stall in the busiest market place in the world. It's now possible to sell and buy just about anything over the World Wide Web. Even this...

WWW=World Wide Wee

An American called Kenneth Curtis started a business selling his own urine on the Internet (and customers used their "Pee See" browsers to find his site). Various authorities, like sporting bodies and the police, regularly test people's urine to see if they've been taking drugs. Kenneth decided he would sell people his own entirely drug-free wee so that they could use it when they were taking drug tests and avoid being caught.

The wee was strapped to their bodies in a little container and just to make sure it came out at body temperature Kenneth thoughtfully attached a heating device to it. The police eventually found out about Ken's crafty liddle widdle fiddle and arrested him. Kenneth was really put out and said, "If you can't sell urine over the web, what can you sell?"

But what do you do if you've bought something on the Net then decided you don't want it? You auction it of course. On the Internet!

The biggest bring and buy sale in cyberspace

The most famous of these Internet auction sites is eBay.com. There are usually around 20,000 items for sale on the site on any one day and thousands of people wander around the eBay market place looking at what's up for grabs. Of course, with so much stuff for sale, strange items are bound to crop up every now and again. Take a look at this list and decide which have actually been offered for sale on eBay, and which are the…

World Wide Wind-ups?

ⓐ A MONGOLIAN BEARD CRIMPER

ⓑ ADOLF HITLER'S MOUSTACHE

ⓒ A BIT OF THE MOON

ⓓ SOME MAGGOTS

ⓔ A STUFFED GIRAFFE

ⓕ A HUMAN KIDNEY

ⓖ A BUMPER-SIZED PACKET OF SQUASHED-FLY BISCUITS (CONTAINING REAL FLIES)

FLY BICS

ⓗ A TRANSPARENT TOILET SEAT WITH RARE COINS EMBEDDED IN IT

(i) A TIN OF ELBOW GREASE

(j) OLIVER CROMWELL'S WOODEN FALSE TEETH

(k) A SURFACE-TO-AIR GUIDED MISSILE

(l) SOME GHOST POOP

(m) A STUFFED DEER'S BOTTOM (TO GO ON THE WALL)

(n) A PURSE MADE OUT OF THE HEAD AND BODY OF A REAL FROG

(o) A SNUFF CONTAINER MADE FROM A RAM'S HEAD ON WHEELS

Answers:

a) True. **b)** False – Hitler's moustache was burned by his servant (along with rest of him) after he committed suicide in 1945. **c)** True. **d)** True. **e)** True. **f)** True – In February 2000 someone advertised their kidney for sale on eBay and said it could be picked up in the Swiss city of Zurich. Not long afterwards someone bid over $6,000 for it but eBay stopped the sale. **g)** False. **h)** True. **i)** False. **j)** False. **k)** True. **l)** True – Actually it was bits of foam packaging in a bag with a label saying "ghost poop". **m)** True – Someone paid $90 for it. **n)** True. **o)** True.

gagaga.com

One American couple put adverts on various Internet auction sites offering big businesses the opportunity to name their new baby. Their idea was that the businesses would jump at the chance to have human beings named after them. The kids would be nothing less than walking advertisements. The couple were hoping that a big corporation might pay around £300,000 for the privilege. Just imagine the consequences...

You'll be relieved to know that there were no takers for the couple's wacky scheme, so they ended up calling their baby Zane!

Cyberbyte
"Watch" out! There's a big "time" conman about

A man from Sunderland in the north-east of England saw a photograph of a magnificent Rolex watch offered for sale on the eBay Internet auction site. He thought it would make a timely birthday present for his wife so he bid £5,000 for it. His bid was accepted and he was delighted (second-hand Rolex watches normally go for around £12,000) so he sent off the dosh. Not long afterwards he received a photograph of the watch in the post. Realizing that all was probably not quite as it should be he complained to the seller. The man emailed him back to say that's all he was getting as he'd bid for the photo and not a real Rolex watch.

Properly e-dressed

When TV first came out people used to dress up to watch it because they believed that the bods on the telly could actually see into their homes and naturally they wanted to look their best for them. In the age of the Incredible Internet, people are slightly more clued up about technology and wear whatever they want to surf the sites. In 2000 a search-engine company wanted to find out what people in Britain wore when they were surfing, so they asked the National Opinion Poll company to interview 1,000 people. These are some of the statistics they came up with:

1. The most popular outfit for cyber travel was T-shirt and jeans, with between 60% and 70% of people living in London, East Anglia and Wales going for the scruff-bag look.

2. 27% of women living in the south-west of England said they often just wore their undies while they were emailing friends, chatting or shopping online.

3. 46% of people living in the Midlands said they wore their pyjamas when they went online.

4. 8% of people in Yorkshire said they actually stripped off completely before they logged on.

OK! Time to slip into your jeans and T-shirt (or jim jams) and get online for the…

Cyberspace surfari

Ten WWWWWS
(Wild and Wacky World–Wide–Websites)

1. www.let-me-stay-for-a-day.com

A Dutch journalism student wanted to travel around the world but didn't have enough dosh to pay for hotels and what not, so he set up this website asking the world's netizens to put him up for a night. The student, whose name is Ramon Stoppelenberg got hundreds of invitations and started his journey on the 1st May 2001. He keeps a daily diary of all the things that happen to him and the people he meets and you can read about all his adventures on the site. Maybe Ramon doesn't know it yet but all the people who have been so kind to him will no doubt be expecting to have the favour returned.

HI, RAMON. WE WERE WONDERING IF YOU COULD PUT US ALL UP FOR THE NIGHT?

2. www.allmylifeforsale.com

An American artist called John Freyer owed his bank $5,000 so he decided to put everything he owned up for sale on the Internet. Fifty friends came round to his house to help him sort hundreds and hundreds of his treasured bits and bobs then he listed them all on his site. Things he's sold so far include a pink shirt, 12 taco shells

and a pair of baseball boots. When he's finally flogged everything off John will auction his website name, then go on a huge tour of America visiting all his old possessions.

3. www.hatsofmeat.com

Take a butcher's at this juicy cyber-joint. It's packed with photos of hats made from meat, ranging from a porkpie hat (of course) to a sizzlingly stylish bacon hat with a chin strap of sausages. If you feel desperate to have your own meat hat, a short video shows you how to make a "basebull" cap from steak. Advice to vegetarians: give this one the chop!

4. www.icepick.com

A Dutch couple called Karen and Alex and their cat, Sparky, have been recording almost everything that happens in their house in Holland since 1998. If you like, you can visit their site and see how their webcam captures every heart-stopping moment of their fascinating and totally chilling "fridge-door-opening sequence". (Calm down, you've not even been yet!) Or, if you're looking for real excitement, you can scan their utterly gripping statistics pages. For example, if you'd visited on 4th August 2001 you would have discovered that the same fridge door had been opened a total of 17,611 times since 12th June 1998 at an average opening time of 37.38656873 seconds. However if those sort of statistics are just too, *too* exciting for you, you could just watch the completely stunning front-door bell webcam, marvel at the family cat visiting its food bowl or check out when the toilet was last flushed.

5. www.worstcasescenarios.com

The website for nervous folk (or ones who like to live dangerously). On this site you can find out how to get out of all sorts of dangerous situations. It includes tips on what to do if you're attacked by a shark, stuck in quicksand or inconvenienced by a non-opening parachute.

NOW, WHAT WAS THE URL OF THAT WEBSITE?

6. freeweb.pdq.net/headstrong

This brilliant site, otherwise known as Bizarre Stuff You Can Make In Your Kitchen, is crammed with great experiments and things to make and do. Included amongst the loads of peculiar projects for potty people are: masses of great recipes for designer slime; how to give an egg a "see-through" shell; how to fit a hard-boiled egg into a narrow-necked bottle; and the infinitely tasteful, but somewhat mind warping, how to make a false shrunken head. Warning! Some of the projects are slightly complicated and a teensy bit dangerous so you'll definitely need to get a grown up to help you with them.

7. www.mirrorimage.com/air/page05.html

This groovy site tells you everything you ever wanted to know about the mysterious instrument known as the air guitar, i.e. the invisible guitar that sad grown-ups and over excitable teenagers are fond of playing in front of bedroom mirrors or at wild parties. It tells you things like how to play air guitars really well, how to hold them and how to use them for different sorts of music such as jazz, rock and easy listening. It even has air guitars for sale and quotes from the satisfied musicians who've bought them.

8. www.smilie.com/digimask_done.php3

Get "ahead" in cyberspace by scanning in or sending two digital photos of your head to this site and filling in the vital statistics form. They'll make you a speaking, 3D "Digimask" screen model of your head in just minutes. Then it's yours to do want you want with: email it to your friends; use it

to try on products like specs and wigs when web shopping; wear it to chat rooms; or become a cyber grappler by transferring your virtual face to one of the maulers in an online wrestling game.

9. www.animalmummies.com/adoptfiles/list. html

This site gives you the opportunity to adopt an Egyptian mummy. Not the human sort but cute animal mummies like cats, crocodiles and dogs. All these ancient artefacts need looking after if they aren't going to crumble to dust so your contribution goes to preserving them. It costs about £60 to adopt a mummified dog, £30 for a fish and £15 for a crocodile egg.

By the way, if you don't fancy the mummy you could adopt a nice living cow for about £28 at the Dutch website www.adopteereenkoe.nl.

10. www.setiathome.ssl.berkeley.edu

This one has been set up by scientists who want to find out if there really is intelligent life in outer space. Masses of unidentified radio signals are bleeping away out there but there are just so many of them that it's impossible for the boffins to check them all and identify the tell-tale patterns that

SIGH

BLEEPB LEEPBL EEPBLE EPBLEE P - ETC...

could mean they're being sent by intelligent alien beings. What they've done (the scientists, not the aliens) is enlisted the help of surfers around the world. So far, half a million volunteers have logged on and are helping with this huge number-crunching project. You can join in if you want to. You don't have to be an expert; your PC will do the work of sorting out all the bits of info they get from radio telescopes and you'll get a snazzy screen saver that shows how the job's progressing.

THIS CAN'T BE AN INTELLIGENT BEING

"TYK ME TWO YORE LEEEDUR"

Cyberbyte
Digital deprivation – part one

Some people look at some *very* weird sites on the Internet. One man was looking at a site containing some really gruesome photos when he spotted a set of severed fingers and thought...

HEY I RECOGNIZE THEM!

He couldn't quite put his finger on who the pinkies belonged to but he printed off a photo and showed it to his pal who recognized them immediately. Because they were his! He'd lost them in a factory accident some months earlier. He remembered that a member of the medical team who'd treated him had asked if he could have a snap of his pulverized pinkies. Some people ... they've got their sticky little fingers into everything!

Closer than you think!

Try and create a mental map of all of the millions of sites that are on the Web, then try and imagine how they're all interconnected by all those zillions of hypertext links. Brains trickling out of your ears yet? It's a mind-boggling image, isn't it? But not quite as mind-boggling as you might suppose! When the World Wide Web had reached the point where it had more than 800 million sites on it, an inquisitive techno-bod let his pet software robot loose in the WWW and said something like...

He wanted to discover information about the "interconnectivity" of all the sites on the World Wide Web. In other words, how they were all linked. The "bot" went scampering off into cyberspace, then began thrusting its cold wet nose into lots and lots of different web pages. As it got to each one it examined all the page's possible hypertext links then followed each one of those to its destination.

It carried on doing this until it had nosed around something like a third of a million sites. After that, various big-brained individuals did squillions and squillions of incredibly complicated calculations and came up a with an astonishing discovery. They worked out that, even though the Web has got a humungous amount of documents on it, on average, any two randomly selected web pages are only 19 clicks apart!

THE REALLY ANNOYING "POP-UP" CHAPTER

Some people are absolutely addicted to the Internet and spend their spare hours surfing themselves silly, others don't know a mouse from a modem, while a whole lot more come somewhere between these two extremes. Which category do you fit into? Answer this simple questionnaire and find out whether you're...

A webaholic, a nerd ... or a newbie?

1. If you saw a mouse (furry sort) would you...

a) grab hold of it and attempt to plug its tail into the USB port of your PC?

b) offer it a piece of virtual cheese?

c) stand on a chair and scream?

2. How do you think of your parents?

a) A rather dull (but useful) website known as www.mum-and-dad.com.

b) A couple of items of unreliable software which always seem to crash at exactly the wrong moment.

c) A couple of very nice (but sad) left-overs from those primitive technical dark ages known as the 1980s.

3. How many hours a day do you spend surfing the Net?

a) Buzz off … can't you see I'm surfing the Net!

b) Between one and three.

c) What's a Net?

4. Have you ever…

a) tried to sprinkle salt on your postman?

b) looked in the bathroom mirror and mistaken yourself for an emoticon? ☺

c) tried to use a rubber eraser to get rid of an email spelling error on your PC screen?

5. Do you think that computers might one day take over the world?

a) Just a minute … I'll ask my computer what it thinks.

b) We'll always remain in control.

c) What's a computer?

6. What would you like for Christmas?

a) Fifteen gigabytes of extra memory to be surgically implanted into your brain.

b) A really snazzy new PC.

c) Some chocolate fudge and a squeaky toy.

7. Have you ever…

a) tried to "download" the contents your best friend's brain?

b) wondered which bit of your pet cat you put the batteries in?

c) attempted to stick a stamp on an email?

8. Have you ever…

a) taken your PC to bed with you and cuddled it like a teddy?

b) worn your swimming costume to surf the Web?

c) asked where the toilet is when visiting an Internet chat room?

9. Where is cyberspace?

a) In our heads.

b) California.

c) About three miles north of Jupiter.

10. If there was a sudden electricity cut in your street when you were surfing the Internet, would you…

a) continue to stare vacantly at your PC screen, wildly tapping your keyboard and clicking away at your mouse as if nothing had happened, even if the power cut went on for weeks and weeks?

b) dash round to PC World and continue surfing on one of their computers until the crisis was over?

c) play with your squeaky toy for a while?

How you scored:

Mainly a's – Webaholic ... no doubt about it! You're definitely the sort of person whose idea of a brilliant time would be to spend a month on a desert island with Tim Berners-Lee discussing tangential interface encryption. You're probably absolutely brilliant at HyperText Mark-up Language but completely unable to clean your own teeth or comb your hair without falling over at least three times.

Mainly b's – Nerd ... with possible webaholic tendencies You're obviously utterly nuts about computers and the Internet. You might even be in the habit of giving your PC an affectionate hug and a kiss on the cheek before closing it down for the night.

However, when visiting Internet chat rooms you may still have a tendency to wear your best clothes in the hope that you will meet someone really fantastic. Oh dear, you really ought to get out more.

Mainly c's – Bit of a newbie (but don't ask which bit) ... or possibly a complete techno-twit! Come to think of it, it's a miracle you were able to work out how to open this book! You're more than likely the sort of person who thinks that "modem" is what shop assistants call posh ladies, and that "pixels" are the little fairy folk who live inside computers and make them work.

If you accidentally downloaded a "virus" from the Internet you'd probably put your PC to bed and dose it with cough medicine and cod liver oil.

By the way, for those who *aren't* in the know:
a) a **modem** is the thing that converts digital data so that it will flow smoothly down a telephone line.
b) pixels are the tiny dots that make up pictures and whatnot on your computer screen.

THE POST WITH THE MOST

Email is short for "electronic mail". In just a few years it's changed the lives of millions of people, postmen (and dogs) around the world.

It's fast, cheap, efficient, easy to use, and it can be tons of fun. It helps people keep in touch with friends, family and fellow workers all over the place. At the click of a mouse, messages are whizzed thousands of kilometres across the planet (or hundreds of centimetres across office floors) and delivered into computer mail-boxes more or less instantaneously.

Like lots of other things connected with the Incredible Internet, email wasn't invented by one single person but came about as a result of projects carried out by different people. But this pair are probably the most important of them all...

Lo ... and behold! It's the world's first-ever email!

The world's first-ever computer-generated electronic message was sent in 1969 by L Kleinrock (an American computer Professor, not a German pop group) and some of his students from his laboratory at the University of California in Los Angeles. His idea was to try and send a message to another local network computer at a research centre in San Francisco. The first thing he had to do was to get the two computers to acknowledge each other, or "shake hands", as some people say. To do this he had to type LOGIN. This is what happened…

So the world's first ever email said LO! However, the Prof and his pals weren't to be beaten. They did it again, and this time it worked! But don't forget! This message was only between two computers in a *local* network, not a wider network like the Internet would eventually become. Someone else was going to dream up a way of doing that.

Really important tip for those new to email: When you send an email nowadays it's not necessary to actually ring your friend every time you type in each letter of your message in order to check they've received it. Things have come on quite a way since then, all thanks to people like Prof Kleinrock ... and this man:

QWERTYUIOP

In 1971 a computer engineer called Ray Tomlinson, (not Qwertyuiop) devised a way of sending email to other machines on a *network* of computers. Just to make sure it worked he sent his first message from one machine to another one that was in the same room. It said QWERTYUIOP. Why? Because he was a huge fan of the Flowerpot Men. No, not really! It was because he was anxious to get his test up and running and as qwertyuiop are the first row of letters on a keyboard, that was the easiest thing to type. But Ray knew he had to come up with a way of indicating that his message was heading out to a computer, or computers, in the bigger network, rather than just going to a local group of computers. He needed a symbol that was simple and catchy and couldn't be confused with other letters. So he had a quick think…

The @ .... what's <u>yours</u> called?

All thanks to Ray's bright idea back in 1971, every time you send an email you now have to use that little "@" symbol with its tail curling back around itself, making it look like a sparrow's-eye view of a sleeping cat. Boring people all over the place call it the "at" symbol ... but do you know where it came from originally?

The @'s been around for yonks and before Ray decided to incorporate it into Internet email addresses it was mainly used by people like number crunchers and shopkeepers whenever they wanted to indicate how much items cost or weighed. For example they'd write something like "6 bags of grain @ £10 each". No one's entirely sure who first dreamed up the @ but it's thought that it originated hundreds of years ago, long before printing presses were invented. In those days books were produced by monks who spent hours and hours laboriously copying them out, then copying them out again ... and again. They are said to have shortened "at" to @ to make the job easier. It doesn't sound like much but if you're writing all day long for almost every day of your life it makes a big difference.

@ ... available at a pet shop near you

The @ has got tons of different names in lots of languages but almost all of them seem to associate its shape with some sort of animal. Here are some of the different names for the @. What's your favourite?

Now that almost every country in the world is on the Net people are thinking up a world wide name for the @ that is recognized by everyone. Ideas they've had so far include "vortex", "arobase", "whorl", "schnable" and "snail"! (Why not just "curly"?)

Triffic traffic!

Most people think that email is the best thing since sliced trees. The number sent just grows and grows (while postmen's rounds get smaller and smaller)...

1998 – Four trillion (that's four million million million million) emails were sent in the United States of America. But only 15% of the population were online!

It was also estimated that a typical busy American office worker had to deal with over 100 emails a day.

1999 – It was estimated that the number of emails being sent in the UK was doubling every 100 days.

2000 – 10 billion emails were being sent worldwide every single day!

2005 – Experts have estimated that over 35 billion emails will be sent worldwide every day. Staggering, isn't it? By the way, if you'd like to comment on these statistics, feel free to drop us an email at ... swamptheworldwithunnecessaryemails @maketheserviceprovidersevenricherthan ever.com.

Better by letter?

Not everyone loves email. A 64-year-old politician in Holland probably wished people like Ray and Leonard hadn't gone to the trouble of inventing electronic mail. He just couldn't get his head around the stuff and was soon overwhelmed by the newfangled emails that began pouring into his office as the great new invention began to catch on.

He had so much difficulty using the email software on his computer that council officials eventually took pity on him. Using ye olde pen and paper they painstakingly turned every single one of the poor old technophobe's incoming emails into good old handwritten letters!

E-rror terror

In 2001 it was said that on average an office worker would send at least 50 emails a day. And half of them would be to people sitting less than ten feet away. It was also said that half the emails sent were unnecessary.

Anyway, necessary or not, that would be thousands of emails per person per year. When you're clicking and sending that many it's more or less inevitable that you're going to make mistakes, like this pair of prize bloomers...

Message sent. Ooer!

1. The boss of a publishing company who was attending a technology conference accidentally sent an email to all the other people attending telling them they were...

2. Most people like to keep how much they earn a secret, especially from their fellow workers (it's a grown-up thing – you'll soon get the idea). The boss of a big company accidentally emailed all his workers with the details of how much everyone else in the firm was earning. When he realized the daft thing he'd done he thought he better take quick action.

So! What do you think he did?

a) Sent them all another email saying it was a joke.

b) Set off the fire alarm.

c) Jumped straight out of the window.

d) Sacked himself.

QUICK, MAN, THINK! IF YOU CAN SORT THIS MESS OUT YOU DESERVE TO GIVE YOURSELF A RISE!

Answer: b) He set off the fire alarm. Then, while everyone was out of the building, he scurried from desk to desk, manually deleting every copy of his email from every computer in the office.

Keep this to yourself!

Don't think that the contents of your emails are just a secret between you and the people you're sending them to. Some Internet Service Providers keep a record of every email ever sent on their system. It's not a problem. If they can store billions of pages of data, a few squillion emails or so are no problem.

But, even more scary than that ... Big Brother is watching you! Not the telly programme but the US military. If you go anywhere near the huge RAF base at Menwith Hill in Yorkshire you'll undoubtedly spot 20 massive "golf balls" on a hillside. They weren't left there by a giant Tiger Woods.

They're the monitoring antennae that form part of the American government's "Echelon" surveillance system ... the biggest electronic snooping centre in the world. It's reported that the people operating them are able to read millions of private emails relayed by satellite systems.

So when you send your next email, just be careful. Especially regarding what you say about all those bigwig generals and windbag politicians. Oh, and by the way, if you do want to email those politicians directly, or maybe a few superstars, here are a few e-dresses to be going on with.

Drop 'em a line

Prime Minister of Britain, Tony Blair: tonyblair@geo2.opotel.org.uk

President of the USA: president@whitehouse.gov

Steven Spielberg, film director: ssberg@amblin.com

Clint Eastwood, filmstar: rowdiyates@aol.com

Madonna, pop star: madonna@ubr.com

Bill Gates, computer tycoon: billg@microsoft.com

Warning: These are "official" websites so you won't necessarily get a personal reply from the celeb in question. And remember! Some famous bods change their email addresses more frequently than their undies, so you may get your post returned (or an invite to Number 10?).

Absolutely FONTabulous!

A psychologist took a look at the different fonts that people used for their emails and decided that it was possible to tell something about their personalities from the typeface they chose for their messages. See if you can match the font to the characteristics of the type of person who, according to the study, is most likely to use it:

1. Courier
2. Helvetica
3. Georgia
4. Comic sans
5. *Handwriting*
6. Times
7. Arial

a) Old fogey, stuck in the past.
b) Fashion conscious and groovy.
c) Overly-familiar and over-friendly.
d) Modern and up-to-date – knows what's going on in the world.
e) Attention seeking, pain in the neck.
f) Trustworthy and in touch with what's what.
g) Safe and trustworthy – like sensible shoes.

Answers: 1. a) 2. d) 3. b) 4. e) 5. c) 6. f) 7. g)

According to the study, Prince Charles uses modern Helvetica to show he's in touch with current issues and has his ears to the ground (obviously quite easy for him) while the Governor of the Bank of England, uses Courier because he's a traditionalist who misses the "good old days" (and it's the only one that works on his PC).

Cybertip! Use a different font for every email you send. That way you won't get ... typecast!

Cyberbyte
So easy, even a gorilla can use it!

On 27th April 1998 a 27-year-old gorilla called Koko went online for an "inter-species" computer chat. People were invited to email their questions to Koko, who can understand 2,000 words of English and has been learning sign language since the age of two. Koko's teacher read the emailed questions, communicated them in sign language, then someone tapped out Koko's replies on the

computer's keyboard. When someone asked Koko what she wanted for her birthday she replied "food and smokes". But she didn't want cigarettes! Smoke was the name of her pet kitten. Aah! Koko has her own website at www.koko.org where you can see her and her kitten.

E-rage!

When people were first getting connected to the Internet, receiving their first email was often a big occasion about which they would get really excited.

However, now that office workers are getting dozens of them every single day, emails are no longer anything to ~~write~~ ... *email* home about. In fact, people are now getting so much electronic post that it's driving them round the bend. The International Stress Management Association say that emails are now among the top 20 causes of stress, along with traffic jams, money worries, and marriage problems (and constantly being asked questions by the International Stress Management Association).

When a computer company interviewed over 4,000 people about how they behaved with their computers, one in four of them admitted that getting oodles of emails sometimes made them so angry that they flipped their lids and actually *attacked* their computers! And a quarter of young office workers said they had seen people kick computers. Obviously a case for the RSPCPC! (Royal Society for the Prevention of Cruelty to Personal Computers.)

johnsmith@internet.com?

Have you got an email address? Unless you happen to be called Hyperbole Spink, Dredge Polygon or Zane Buffalodump, you'll probably realize that at least one other person in the world has got the same name as you. Unlike with domain names, other Internet users can't threaten to sue you for having the same name as them but it can cause problems when you're trying to set up an email address for the first time. For example, if you happen to be called David Jones you might well be struggling as there are already 15,671 David Joneses in Britain alone. If you're a girl called Margaret Smith your problem won't be quite so bad because there are a mere 7,640 of you in the UK.

Awesome email

Not everyone uses email for sending boring, "Thank you for your email thanking me for my email" messages. Imaginative individuals all over the place have thought up all sorts of original uses for cyberpost. Here are three of them...

1. Dead useful An artist in Holland (yes, the digitally demented Dutch again) has designed an online tomb that allows a dead person's family and friends to email messages to their coffin then get messages back from them. Obviously it helps no end if the deceased actually programmes in their messages before they die. If they don't and their loved ones *do* receive a message, they know there's something seriously spooky going on.

2. It's in the Net! The EVV Eindhoven Dutch football team are letting their fans email them advice during matches. (It'll save a fortune in throat sweets.) While a match is taking place they can send the players ideas via their coach and manager. The advice will include things like who should take a penalty, who should be brought on as substitutes and which members of the opposing team should be marked (or viciously tripped up). And in addition to that, the fans will be able to suggest which players should be bought or sold (but preferably not while they're in the middle of scoring a goal).

3. Drop us a line A teacher and his class of eight-year-olds at a school in Nebraska in the United States decided to do a geography project based on the Internet. They sent out 25 emails and asked people to reply to them so they could pinpoint where the responses had come from. So how many replies do you think they got?

a) none

b) 100

c) 1,000

d) 110,000

Answer: d) Yes, instead of getting just a few dozen like they'd expected the kids received over *one hundred and ten thousand* emails! And as well as the emails they got *six hundred* letters and parcels too! One woman in Australia even sent them a box full of toy koala bears and books about her country. And a NASA scientist sent them an email accompanied by a load of photographs of the earth taken from outer space.

NOW THEN CLASS, THIS MORNING WE'LL BE WRITING ONE HUNDRED AND TEN THOUSAND THANK YOU LETTERS!

Cyber-tip
Don't lick ... just click!

You probably don't have any trouble at all whizzing emails off all over the place but maybe your grandparents (or parents?) don't feel entirely comfortable with the idea of sending electronic letters. If this is the case, put them at their ease by recommending the www.wonderstamp.com/suite.html website to them. It's got a whole load of snazzy stamps that can all be downloaded for free on to emails giving them that more traditional look that's associated with snail mail. You never know, once you've had a look at the site yourself you might even fancy decorating your own e-post with the "virtual" stamps including subjects like art, nature, sport, flowers and special occasions.

Email can sometimes bring Internet users ginormous problems. They're often the sort that are sent by the people you're going to read about in the next chapter...

HACKERS, CRACKERS, TRACKERS ... AND OODLES OF SMACKERS

Hackers and crackers are people who get access to the information on other people's computers or websites without being given permission to do so. It's a bit like having someone sneak into your house then steal your ideas and possessions, or simply make a right mess of things while they're in there. However, instead of breaking a window or forcing a lock to gain entry, hackers and crackers use all manner of crafty tricks to discover the vital passwords that will give them access to other people's files and programs.

Hacking on the Internet really took off around the time the World Wide Web was created because many of the newly created websites and email addresses presented hackers with lots of challenging new cyberspace break-in opportunities they just couldn't resist. In no time at all they were setting up their own websites where they passed on tips, news and details of their latest astounding hacks. No sooner had lots of web-wise whizz kids set up stacks of supposedly secure sites on the Internet than lots more web-wise whizz kids started trying to get into them. They could steal information, interfere with their running efficiency or simply feel really pleased with themselves for having wriggled their way past all the security devices. In order to get your head around the idea of hacking it might first be a good idea to learn a bit of...

Hacketty yack (or how to speak "hack")

Crackers Guaranteed to cheese everyone off. These are hackers with a really bad attitude. They are the sort that deliberately crash systems out of sheer spitefulness using viruses (often attached to emails). They also blackmail ISPs (Internet Service Providers) by threatening to bring their systems to a standstill with "quack attacks" if they don't hand over dollops of dosh.

SO WHAT'S A "QUACK ATTACK" THEN?

Thought you'd never ask...

Quack attacks These are attacks on big websites like Yahoo and Amazon. The sites are said to be "sitting ducks" because crackers can bombard them with so many requests for information that they suffer huge data traffic jams which eventually cause them to seize up.

YES. SEE WHAT YOU MEAN!

HONK! HONK! BEEP BEEP!

COME ON, HURRY UP!

GET A MOVE ON!

Hackers Hackers see themselves as more decent bods who don't do their hacking for money *or* because they've got a mean streak!

They say they hack to show up gaps in computer security systems or just because they enjoy the challenge of finding a way into a system. Some of them regard themselves as knights in shining armour who wander around cyberspace doing good deeds.

IT IS I! SIR CYBERLOT... DEDICATED TO RESCUING MODEMS IN DISTRESS!

Script kiddies This is what some people call junior hackers who only know a few computer languages. They don't particularly like people calling them this and will often do bad things to the websites of anyone who does so.

SHE HASN'T SAID HER FIRST WORD YET BUT SHE'S A WHIZZ AT LINUX AND HTML!

TAP TAP

Pinging Involves sending a simple message (like "Gotcha!"?) to another computer then getting it to "bounce" back to you just to make sure you've established the necessary communication to do your hacking.

Zombies This is the name given to computers which are taken over by crackers so they can use them to break into big computer sites without being identified. In other words they're a bit like stolen cars that are used to carry out bank raids.

There are thousands and thousands of hackers lurking out there in cyberspace. Some of them have carried out such astonishing Internet hacks that their exploits have now become quite legendary. Let's meet three of them by sneaking into the...

111

Hackers hall of fame

The Analyzer
Real name: Ehud Tenebaum
Claim to fame: Along with two other Israeli and two American teenage hackers Ehud hacked his way into the computers at the world famous American military headquarters known as the

Pentagon and stole military software programs (and a top General's best fighting boots). Altogether he broke into 200 computers around the world including ones at NASA (the American space exploration organization) and the Israeli parliament. He also destroyed the websites of two anti-Israeli terrorist groups. The Israeli people saw him as a sort of modern-day Robin Hood and even the Israeli Prime Minister described him as a great computer whizz kid.

ROBIN! YOU'RE THE EHUD TENEBAUM OF THE TWELFTH CENTURY!

What he does now: Ehud is the chief technology officer at a computer consulting firm. (Naturally!)

Condor

Real name: Kevin Mitnick

Claim to fame: When they see Kevin coming, computers in their thousands run and hide in cupboards. To describe Kevin as clever would be like saying that the Empire State Building is quite tall. When he was a lad  he couldn't afford a PC so he used to go into computer shops and use their demonstration models to call up other computers on the Internet. Later on he became a serial hacker and as a result of all his hacktivities he managed to get his mug on an FBI "Most Wanted" poster. Amongst his various hacks and cracks he nicked 20,000 credit card numbers. After going on the run and successfully pretending to be someone else Kevin was eventually tracked down and put in prison for five years.

What he does now: Kevin's out of clink but he's banned from using a computer or a mobile phone or even from working for anyone who has a computer in their building! Aaaah!

Find out more on ... www.kevinmitnick.com.

Vladimir Levin

Real name: Vladimir Levin

Claim to fame: In the good old days when life was simple, robbing banks involved pulling a pair of tights over your head, brandishing a water pistol and yelling, "Stick em up!" as you prayed your getaway coach hadn't been wheelclamped. No longer! Using the Incredible Internet, it's now possible to steal humungous amounts of money from banks all around the world without even leaving the comfort of your own armchair. But only if you've got the know-how of someone like Vladimir. In 1994, from their cosy offices in Russia, bad Vlad and his pals shifted a (Vladi) mere ten million dollars from customers' accounts at the huge Citibank in America. They did it simply by staying late after work and doing a few handy hacks on their laptop computers. Fortunately for Citibank and its customers they were caught before they had time to spend much of the money and all but $400,000 was recovered.

I KNOW IT'S NOT NECESSARY TO LOOK LIKE THIS, BUT IT'S MUCH MORE THRILLING!

Cyberbyte
Doh! A 401 over a 141 leads to a 1471 followed by a 999

Using his remarkable computer skills a 15-year-old schoolboy hacked into the site of an Internet company and discovered some of their most closely guarded business secrets. He then telephoned them, saying he would pass on all the information to their competitors if they didn't give him a great dollop of dosh. Unfortunately for him, when he contacted the company with his blackmail demand, the boy didn't use his remarkable telephone skills (or, as most people would say, common sense). He phoned the company from a home phone line and forgot to dial 141 before making his call which would have meant that he couldn't be traced. As it was, the person taking his call simply dialled 1471, got his phone number and sent the cops to his house.

A hacker's tale – the curious case of Curador

Not all youthful hackers are as careless as that schoolboy. Some are so smart that they manage to run rings round the most experienced crimebusters in the world.

WINTER 2000

HUGE INTERNATIONAL CYBER-HEIST BY HORDE OF HARDENED HACKERS!

Breaking news from our Internet Correspondent, WW Webster

Panic on the streets!

It's panic stations! 23,000 credit card numbers have been stolen by a gang of top international computer criminals. The effects have been devastating. It's estimated that the hackers have already done **two million pounds**' worth of damage to the Internet industry! An Internet e-commerce company has been driven out of business and top credit card company, Visa International, has had to spend a **quarter of a million** pounds upgrading its security! Included amongst the stolen credit card numbers is one belonging to the richest man in the world!

SHUCKS! SOMEONE STOLE MY COTTON PICKIN' CREDIT CARD NUMBER AND USED IT TO BUY ME A LOAD OF STUFF I DIDN'T NEED!

BILL GATES

NEWS OF THE NERDS

A bit later in WINTER 2000

RAMPAGE OF MYSTERY COMPUTER CRIMINALS CONTINUES

by WW Webster

The mystery mob of computer masterminds are still wreaking havoc in the world of international finance! E-commerce sites and banks are being broken into all over America, Canada, Thailand and Britain.

The situation is so serious that the authorities have called in the big guns! The FBI, Interpol, the Royal Canadian Mounted Police, the British police and even cops from the Far East are meeting as I write.

But they are still completely clueless as to the identity of the criminals. All they know is that it's obviously the work of a hardened gang of big-time cyber-crooks using oodles of sophisticated state-of-the-art computer equipment.

HACKER-TRACKER HOT ON TRAIL OF MR BIG AND HIS BOYS

by WW Webster

STOP PRESS!

After spending almost two weeks searching for clues to Curador's true identity Chris, the cyber-sleuth, has cracked the case! And he's now spent 48 sleepless hours putting together a report of his findings for the FBI and the police.

At last! A breakthrough in the hunt for the havoc-wreaking hackers. Chris Davis, a Canadian ex-hacker and computer security consultant, has found a clue on a hacker website. The gang's Mr Big has posted messages on the Internet boasting of his hacks. Apparently he calls himself "Curador". Chris is now hot on his trail!

IT'S ALL QUITE SIMPLE REALLY. HE'S INTERFACING A 2x4 BLOGSPRITE MODEM WITH 90 GIGABYTE CHIP KEFFWINKLER

PARDON?

WHAT?

NEWS OF THE NERDS

A bit later in SPRING 2000

COPS AND F.B.I. SWOOP ON "CURADOR"!

A NEWS OF THE NERDS EXCLUSIVE by WW Webster

After staking out his hideaway, the police and the FBI have finally nailed the "Mr Big" who has hacked his way into thousands of credit card accounts the world over. Shortly after the dramatic swoop and subsequent arrest of Curador, I obtained the following exclusive interview with Agent X of the FBI.

WWW: You've got him then. Congratulations! So, where was he operating from? A smoke-filled cellar in Shanghai? A fortified mobsters' mansion in Milwaukee?

Agent X: Well, no. Actually, it was his bedroom … in his mum and dad's cottage in Wales.

WWW: *What!* That doesn't sound like a hang-out for a big-time computer crook!

Agent X (going a bit pink): He wasn't a big-time computer crook. He was a teenager called Raphael Gray.

WWW: But what about his gang? Didn't they give you trouble?

Agent X (blushing deeply): Not really. His "gang" was just his best pal.

WWW: Oh? But I bet they had some really snazzy computer kit up there.

Agent X: Er ... no. Just a second-hand PC that cost a few hundred pounds.

WWW: Ha! Do you mean to tell me two lads using a second-hand computer have run rings around some of the most powerful people and organizations in the world?

Agent X (now bright crimson): Shucks ... I gotta quit! I think I can hear my bleeper going.

It was true. The Mr Big turned out to be a Welsh teenager called Raphael Gray. He confessed his crimes but said that he hadn't been doing the hacking to make himself rich...

Curador's confessions

- Raphael says he did the hacking to alert the world to security failures on shopping sites and sees himself as a sort of saint of the cyberworld.

- When people got to know of Raphael's hacking an American contacted him on the Internet and offered him $15 dollars (£10) for each credit card number – i.e. $34,500 dollars (£23,000) for the lot! Raphael turned him down.

- He also said, "Some of the shopping sites were so open to hacking that you could teach your grandmother to do it."

- He admitted that he got something of a thrill as he waited for thousands of credit card numbers to download to his computer.

- His opinion of most computer security forces was that they "couldn't hack their way out of a paper bag".

121

- Raphael says he'd eventually like to turn his skills to designing computer-aided devices that will help disabled people.

Cyberbyte
Lego a go-go!
When Lego launched its Mindstorms robotics kits in 1998 a student hacked into the program then "reverse engineered" it (i.e. found out how it worked, then rebuilt it), after which he posted all he'd discovered on the Internet. Rather than having a right old sulk and hunting down the hacker and others like him, the Lego company decided it would be a good idea to encourage them so they could get them to point out glitches and flaws in their products.

The *dis*information superhighway

The American politician Al Gore may have described the Incredible Internet as the "Information Superhighway" but, just as with newspapers (and tales your teachers tell you), it's not always a good idea to believe all you see and hear on the World Wide Web. The Internet is a perfect place for people who like to play tricks on their fellow surfers. Are you a dozy dupe or a streetwise surfer? Here are six stories that appeared on the Internet. Five of them are false and one is true. Can you distinguish the genuine article from the hoax? And don't forget, lots of people were taken in by these...

Internet hoaxes

What the emails and messages said (more or less):

1. Don't miss the Nike trainer offer! Send your pongy, battered, old Nike trainers back to their factory in Oregon, USA and they'll send you a pair of brand-new ones. Hoax or honest?

WELL, IF IT TURNS OUT TO BE A HOAX I'LL KICK UP A BIT OF A STINK!

2. Don't forget Internet Shutdown Day! (This was from the Interconnected Network Maintenance Staff of the Massachusetts Institute of Technology, USA.) As many people already know, the Internet has to shut down for 24 hours once every year for cleaning. Therefore it will be closed between 12.01 am on 1st April and 12.01 am on 2nd April while powerful Internet search engines look for dead emails and inactive or disused websites then sweep them up and dump them. Please disconnect your computers from the Net and pass on this email to your friends so they can shut their PCs down too. Hoax or honest?

3. Have you heard about the "exploding whale"? (This was a "news" email.) A 45-foot long, dead whale, weighing *eight* tons, has exploded on a beach in Oregon, USA. Onlookers were deluged by ginormous chunks of whale blubber and guts. One lump of whale blubber actually landed on a camper van and crushed it completely. Hoax or honest?

4. Beware of the man-eating bananas! (This was posted by the Mannheim Research Institute.) A load of bananas from Costa Rica infected with *necrotizing facilitis*, or "flesh-eating bacteria" as it's more commonly known, has arrived in America. The bananas have already zapped Costa Rica's monkey population and are highly dangerous. Readers should stop buying and eating bananas for at least three weeks. If you have eaten a banana and notice anything odd happening to your skin you must go to a doctor immediately as the bacteria eats flesh at ... one square centimetre an hour! Hoax or honest?

5. Don't eat "franken-chickens" Kentucky Fried Chicken have renamed themselves KFC because they aren't allowed to use the word "chicken" anymore. The reason for this is that they don't use real chickens in their products but actually breed "genetically manipulated organisms" to save time and to make more money. These new "mutant" chickens have no beaks, feathers or feet and are kept alive by having nutrients squirted into them through plastic tubes. Hoax or honest?

6. Say no to bonsai kittens A Japanese doctor in New York is feeding chemicals to kittens in order to melt their bones then he's fitting them into bottles (just like sailors used to do with model ships). The bottled kittens are then sold to people as decorative art! They're all the rage in places like New Zealand, Japan and Britain. Don't let them catch on here in America! Hoax or honest?

Answers:

1. Hoax. However, people all over the world were so taken in by this offer that they began sending in their tatty trainers to Nike at the rate of up to 200 pairs a day! Rather than sending them fresh footwear, Nike just wrote to them asking if they wanted their shoddy shoes back. Some did actually write back and say "yes"!

2. Hoax. The times and dates were a giveaway ... weren't they?

3. Honest. When people read this email they just assumed it was another whaley silly Internet hoax but on investigation it turned out to be genuine! There was a dead whale on the beach and after a while it began to get a bit whiffy, but as it was so huge no one was quite sure how to shift it. Someone eventually got the bright idea of blowing it up and turning it into little tasty morsels for the sea gulls. The Oregon Highways Department came along with half a ton of dynamite and put it next to the whale. By now, news of the forthcoming big bang had got around and there was quite a crowd gathered, along with reporters from the newspapers and the local TV station.

I THINK I'M GOING TO BLUBBER

BLOP!

Finally the great moment came and, to great cheers from the crowd, the dynamite was detonated and the whale shot skywards. However, a few seconds later the mood of the onlookers changed completely when ginormous chunks of whale blubber and guts began to rain down on them like some gory tropical monsoon. And yes, one lump of whale did actually crush a camper van. If you're the sort who enjoys seeing this kind of gory stuff you can take at squizz at pictures of the exploding whale at www.hackstadt.com/features/whale

4. Hoax.

LOOK! IT'S A MAN-EATING BANANA! ... HA, FOOLED YOU!

5. Hoax. Definitely one for bird brains!

6. Hoax. This one had so many people fooled that it was investigated by the American FBI. But of course, it's absolutely impussible ... isn't it?

I caught it off the Internet!

Have you ever come down with a virus? They mess up your insides, leave you feeling unable to cope and sometimes prevent you chatting with your pals. And that's more or less what they do to computers. However, unlike the virus which you catch from next door's cat a computer virus arrives in the form of a program which can damage the information stored on your PC. Just like a cold is passed from person to person, the virus is passed from computer to computer.

More often than not, viruses are deliberately created and launched by destructive types who enjoy splattering other folks' hard work.

I'M GONNA BE A VIRUS SPREADER WHEN I GROW UP!

At this very moment there are, no doubt, virus creators out there doing their level best to create a program that will worm its way into our computers just when we need @!!β ???α*@ %2τσβ %*1@ *!τ!!β ???

@!!β ???α*@%2τσβ %*1@ *!τ!!β ???@!!β ???α*@ %2τσβ %*1@ ???...

(THREE WEEKS LATER)
Sorry about that! Problem with a virus. But everything's fine now (apart from being behind with this book!).

Virus facts: good and bad

Bad news: About 300 new viruses are created every week.

Good news: Most are harmless.

Bad news: Many viruses arrive in the form of email attachments.

Good news: Normally, if you don't open the attachment the virus can't infect your computer.

Bad news: For some reason people seem to be unable to resist opening attachments even when they know they haven't asked to be sent them in the first place. Which is probably why bugs like the following ones end up playing havoc with their hard drives and flinging away their files...

Good news: Here comes...

THE HEALTHY COMPUTER GUIDE TO VICIOUS VIRUSES

Melissa

Early warning symptom: The arrival of an email saying:

> "Here is that document you asked for... don't show it to anyone else"

How to catch it: Open the attached document.

Effects: Made about a million computers very poorly, causing £50m of damage.

Who spread it: David Smith, an American computer programmer.

The Anna Kournikova virus
Early warning symptom:

How to catch it: Take a peep at Anna.

Effects: Generally messed up people's email software.

Who spread it: A 20-year-old from Sneek (no kidding!) in Holland. He eventually gave himself up.

The Killer From Manila a.k.a. The Love Bug

Early warning symptom:

> ## "I LOVE YOU"
> Kindly check the attached love letter from me!

How to catch it: Open the attachment.

I'VE GOT A LOVE LETTER. BET THEY HAVEN'T. HA!

Effects: Eight times more destructive than Melissa. Caused billions of dollars worth of damage. In the UK, it messed up computer systems at the BBC, Houses of Parliament, *Times* newspaper and some stock market companies.

Who spread it: Two mischievous twenty-somethings in the Philippines.

Digital Doomsday!

Some gloomy computer security experts have predicted that one day a determined group of cyber-terrorists will bring the whole of the Internet crashing to its knees. Not by attacking a few computers here and there but by launching the mother of all viruses at the most powerful and important parts of the network. In other words, the networks *within* the network that keep the whole thing up and running. This could mean that millions of computers and computer networks all over the world might be paralyzed completely, unable to send or receive email, unable to retrieve information and unable to carry out their day-to-day functions. This sort of thing could be brought about by criminals blackmailing the world's governments for oodles of dosh. Or political hot-heads who are determined to dislodge the puffed-up and powerful. Or simply by a computer wizard who's a few gigabytes short of a hard drive. And unlike most other acts of terrorism it could all be put into operation from thousands of kilometres away. The whole of the industrialized world has become so completely dependent on computers that this sort of attack could well lead to the sort of global technological melt down that really cheerful people

refer to as...

The worst-case scenario
A gloomy winter's evening in the year 2005

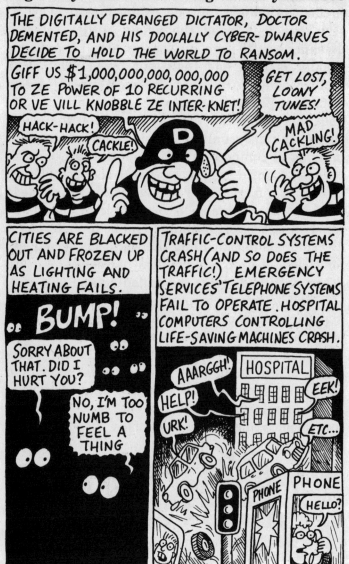

SCHOOLS NETWORKS GO DOWN MAKING LESSONS AN IMPOSSIBILITY.

HURRAH!

HOW TO TEACH WITHOUT A COMPUTER

AIR-TRAFFIC CONTROL COMPUTERS BECOME INOPERABLE LEAVING THOUSANDS OF AEROPLANES UNABLE TO LAND.

OK, WHO'S FIRST?

FOOD AND WATER SUPPLIES ARE DISRUPTED.

DINNER'S READY, CHILDREN

OH NO! NOT BOILED SHOES IN MUD SAUCE AGAIN!

TELECOMMUNICATIONS FAIL EVERYWHERE SO THE WORLD GOVERNMENTS ARE UNABLE TO CO-ORDINATE AN EFFECTIVE RESPONSE (ie, GET THEIR ACT TOGETHER).

HELP!

Grim, or what? So, it's probably time to lighten things up with a...

Cyberbyte

During the summer of 1999 a computer virus prankster sneaked a bug into the computer system of a big Japanese bank. When the bank emailed a news announcement to all of its account holders proudly announcing that it had merged with two more banks it also took the trouble to inform each customer that they were a "stupid jerk".

YOU AIN'T SEEN NOTHING YET!

This chapter is all about the future of the Internet. Some of the things that are being predicted for the coming months and years are so utterly gobsmacking that you may find them harder to believe than this morning's weather forecast. But keep your mind open. The techno trail-blazers of the 21st century are fond of saying that the things the Incredible Internet will make possible are limited only by our imagination (and pocket money). And remember! If you'd time-travelled back to the 16th century and tried to tell folk about telephones, text-messaging and television, they'd say that you were three herrings short of a codpiece and they'd have no doubt "flamed" you for making up porky pies about the world as they knew it.

The shape of nets to come

All sorts of exciting things are about to take place in the world of the Incredible Internet. These are some of the developments that will make them possible.

Canny connections: Totally wireless ... and absolutely tireless!

Look down the back of your computer table and you'll no doubt see something that resembles several snakes having an all-in wrestling match.

Say so long to Internetty spaghetti! Using the same technology that enables people to wander as they please with mobile phones, the webbed world will eventually be entirely wireless.

Disappearing computers: Now you see them ... but soon you won't!

Back in the 1950s computers were almost as big as barns. At the moment desktop computers are around the size of portable tellies, while palmtops and laptops resemble small notebooks and briefcases. It's predicted that by about 2015, palmtops, desktops and laptops will have disappeared altogether.

They'll all have been replaced by micro-computers "embedded" in (i.e. built into) buildings, machines, clothes, and jewellery (and brains?). As a result, objects all over the place will be "alive" with intelligence.

And of course, all of these hidden computers will be linked to the Incredible Internet *all* of the time!

Info in a flash! During the early days of surfing the Internet people often found that it took them ages to log on to websites especially at certain times of the day. This was invariably because thousands of people were all trying to get online at the same time. It was a bit like lots and lots of cars simultaneously attempting to drive down the same narrow road. Next to the new high-power "Broadband" Internet and Internet 2, the original Internet (i.e. Slothnet!) will look like a forest track next to a 12-lane motorway.

Pulverizing PC power! In the next ten years computers will operate thousands of times faster than they do now! By 2015 every PC will be able to receive 100,000 million instructions per second (and they will just be for that little monkey that prances about on your screen saver!).

And, once all that's done and dusted this sort of thing will be a piece of cake...

Beam me up dotty!

Ever since human beings realized that the world was quite a bit bigger than their own front garden, various bods, including scientists and science fiction writers, have dreamed of instantly transporting people from one place to another at the flick of a switch. The idea is known as "teleportation" and, despite the fact that all manner of brainy bods have put their minds to turning it from science fiction to science fact, it looks like the real thing is still a long way off. However, using Incredible Internet technology, web-wizards and cyber-sorcerers have dreamed up the next best thing. It's called "tele-immersion" and it's already being tried and tested. Here's how it works.

Wish you were here?

Imagine you've got two cousins called Tim and Tabitha who just happen to live in Tibet. (You have? What a coincidence!) Tim and Tabitha have got all the tele-immersion kit at their place and you've got it at yours. It's brekky time in Tibet. You link up for a natter and a bit of tele-immersion. Yes! You're going to share their "personal space". This is what happens:

1. The digital cameras and laser range finders in Tim and Tabitha's kitchen constantly do squillions of calculations as they gather visual and positional information about them and the objects around them.

2. As the data's collected, superfast computers break down all the images and the information about what's where and what shape it is, then convert the whole caboodle to a stonking great wodge of three-dimensional geometrical information.

3. This "broken down" information is whizzed across the world on Internet2, just like broken down information packets were transmitted on the old Internet.

4. At your end, the receiving computer reconstructs all the broken-down data then beams it on to a dirty great screen in the form of staggering three-dimensional images. You're wearing a headset that tracks the movements of your head and adjusts the images acccordingly, thus enabling you to "wander" around Tim and Tabitha's place.

5. This data collecting and transmitting process is ongoing. In other words, the computers are constantly calculating and recalculating visual and positional information as Tim and Tabitha scoff their grub, scratch their bottoms and stroke their yak. This involves the computers doing trillions of sums which would even be dead hard for a yak to do but are a doddle for the super-computers of the 21st century.

Being there!

When the first experiments were done with tele-immersion, one of the people taking part said that it felt as if they'd cut a hole in the wall of the room containing the people on view, even though they were masses of miles away. When they leaned forward the people and objects became bigger. They were even able to peer behind the people they were looking at. In the future, tele-immersion will enable people like teams of engineers and architects to work together on projects, even if they're separated by thousands of miles. School children in England will be able to walk along the Great Wall of China peering into the great wastelands of Mongolia while kids in Edinburgh will be able to float along the Amazon with alligators eyeing them greedily, all without actually leaving the comfort and safety of their classroom (the children not the alligators).

145

But the techno time-lords still aren't satisfied. They're now dreaming up ways of enabling you to *feel* Tim and Tabitha (not that you'd want to!). In order for that to happen they're working on the idea of touch simulation, which in geek speak is known as "haptics". (Short for "*happy tickles*"?) So one day, not only will you be able to see Tim and Tabitha in 3D and hear them, but you'll also be able to stroke them (cripes!) *and* (perhaps by using the gizmo described on page 166) you'll be able to smell them too!

Getting really unreal!

Once a computer can produce full-body versions of that 3D "Digimask" you read about on page 82 you could watch yourself starring in your favourite movies or TV soaps.

Some futurologists are now predicting that the Incredible Internet will enable people to live two lives, one real and one imaginary. After a hard day at the office, school or factory, people of the future will simply slip into some sort of "cyber-travel" outfit, then enter interactive "other worlds" created by teams of artists, set designers, actors and writers in just the same way as they plonk themselves in front of today's TV soaps.

The Grid – An Inter-net of computer power

Another thing the web wizards and computer conjurors are working on is something called the Grid. It's a sort of Inter-net of computer power. It's rather similar to the National Electricity Grid that allows different regions to borrow spare leccy from each other. It works like this...

Say you've discovered a brilliant but really complicated game that you're desperate to play but unfortunately your PC doesn't have enough power to support it. However, just down the road your best friend is away on holiday so their PC is standing idle. The Grid would enable your PC to borrow all their PC's unused power.

Of course, the Grid wouldn't be just a street-to-street thing but would be on a world-wide scale and the first people to get to use it would no doubt be bods in industry and science. Despite the fact that individual computer power is increasing at an astonishing rate, the sort of work they're involved in is constantly demanding more and more computer clout. For example, at the CERN laboratories (the place where Tim Berners-Lee dreamed up the World Wide Web) the scientists there are working on something called particle physics which involves them smashing up atoms as if there were no

148

tomorrow (which there probably won't be if it's left to them). As they carry out their atom-smashing experiments they feed all the resulting information into computers which then do their best to try and make sense of what is actually going on (i.e. process all the data). They anticipate that in 2005 they'll be smashing particles at such a rate that raw (unprocessed) information will be gushing out of their smasher-upper machines at a rate equivalent to a million feature-length movies ... *each second*! Now, with dollops of data that big it's going to take an awfully powerful computer to make head and tail of it all. It's just the sort of thing the Grid's power-borrowing system would be ideal for, which is probably why CERN is one of the main centres involved in developing it.

Meet the six-million-megabyte boy and the eight-billion-gigabyte girl

Maybe you've heard people refer to extra brainy bods as "walking computers". Well, it's looking more and more likely that quite soon a lot of us will actually *become* walking computers.

Not quite like this though. At the moment there are tons of portable high-tech gizmos but the problem is that you need at least eight pairs of hands to control them and eight brains to cope with all the information they're capable of bombarding you with.

The idea of the cyber-sorcerers is to combine all of these bits of kit into one simple (ha ha!) multi-functional, "wearable" Internet-linked computer which will be permanently switched on. And it'll be hands free, leaving your mitts available for waving, fly-swatting, taxi-hailing (and unlimited nose-picking). You'll simply control the whole shooting match with your voice.

The first hand-operated (or voice-controlled) wearable computers are already available for people who want to be online all the time. They look like half a pair of specs and they enable wearers to watch the real world with one eye while they gawp at the virtual world with the other.

Just think! You could be walking around Tokyo when you suddenly get an irresistible urge to find out the exact height of Mount Fujiyama or just how many people in Japan own pink tooth brushes or the Japanese for, "Excuse me madam, your car is parked on my left foot." All you do is quickly surf your portable and the info appears in a jiffy. These wearable computers will be incredibly useful for people at work. For example, an engineer working on the logitating wurzle shank of a supersonic aircraft might not be able to remember whether to use a number two or a number three frunge-splocket. Instead of going off to leaf through some technical manual the size of St Paul's Cathedral they'll simply call up the diagram on their eyescreen. Maybe a teacher faced with yet another unanswerable question can use it to astound their pupils!

151

Power to the cyber people

Of course all this portable computing kit will need to be powered. Years ago if you wanted to power high-tech gizmos of this sort you would have been lugging around batteries the size of kitchen sinks. But not any more! Clever cyber-sorcerers have developed clothes made from solar fibres, a bit like the ones used in solar panels. They will convert sunlight to electricity in order to power all of your high-tech kit. You will be able to wander wherever you want and remain connected to the Incredible Internet all of the time. However, it won't be that simple for everyone!

Get lost ... nerd!

Once you've got your wearable computer you need never again worry about being lost. A sliver of silicon (try saying that with a mouth full of toast) embedded in your portable PC would act as a location finder, constantly giving your exact position out on the Internet with pinpoint accuracy, no matter where you were in the world. So, if you were fortunate enough to be skiing in the Alps but *unfortunate* enough to get clobbered by a giant avalanche and buried alive under thousands of tons of St Bernard rescue dogs, the emergency services would be able to find you in a jiffy.

Farmers with huge ranches in places like Australia and America would be able to find lost cows because Internet-linked transmitters clipped to their ears (the cows' ears, not the ranchers') would constantly broadcast their position (or, in the case of the really smart cows, they'd simply phone the ranchers on their mobiles).

The cyber house rules
And of course, if the cyber-salesmen have their way, the places which will be bursting with Internet-linked gizmos will be our own homes...

A PEEP BEHIND THE INTERNET CURTAINS

External doors will be scanned by Internet cameras so that they can be monitored from anywhere around the house or, when the occupants are out, from portable or office computers. To answer the doorbell you won't even have to move.

The kitchen chill-out station with the hottest information

The people who dream up the stuff we-never-knew-we-needed then convince us that we-just-can't-exist-without-it have decided that what-we-all-need-now is one of these.

Maybe you've already got one? In which case you can skip this next bit (and wipe that smug look off your face). Why did the techno-tyrants decide on an Internet fridge rather than an Internet coat hanger or an Internet bottle opener? Well, according to those-who-know-all, the really important things that happen in a house all take place in the kitchen: plans are made, cats give birth to kittens, milk gets spilt, children refuse to eat their greens ... that sort of thing. So the designers decided the kitchen fridge would become an all-thinking, all-knowing Internet access chill-out point.

What does an Internet fridge do? – Some cold hard facts

1. It constantly checks what's put in it and what's taken out then emails the supermarket with a replacement order by scanning bar codes on the goodies.

2. It's a messaging post. Instead of plastering your Internet fridge with post-it notes for your parents you simply email it or write a message on its screen.

3. It's an Internet information station. For example, your fridge can check local traffic conditions in around 200 milliseconds (in case you're thinking of taking it for a spin down the M1).

4. It monitors the weather forecasts. If it hears there's going to be a heat wave over the next few days it automatically lowers its own temperature (and if it discovers there's about to be a hurricane it quickly gathers up all the baby vegetables and goes and hides in the cellar).

5. It's a TV, video, radio and video phone.

6. It's linked to all the other gadgets in your house and it interacts with them. For example, you can use it to control the lights and the central heating. It can also automatically send messages to other appliances.

The Internet fridge is so intelligent and so aware of what's going in your house that it could almost become one of the family. Then again, perhaps not!

Get your set ... it's telly net!

Back in the dark days of 1950s Britain there was only *one* telly channel! And that was only on for a few hours each evening! And in the 1960s as many as 20 million telly watchers would often sit around the goggle box all gawping at the *same* TV programme (not all on the same telly though).

159

But things have changed! Quite soon, and all thanks to the Incredible Internet, a gizmo that's part TV, part hi-fi system, part Internet browser, part radio, part video player (and part golden retriever) will enable us to download thousands of films, pieces of music and books from our chosen online "Internetainment" company. Or even order movies and music straight from the studios. There'll be thousands of TV channels and squillions and squillions of programmes to choose from. In addition to which there'll be 50 or 60 years' worth of old stored programmes to watch. The choice will be mind-boggling.

But don't panic! Your "telly net" machine will sift through all the programmes and do the choosing for you. Once it's learned to recognize your voice and you've told it what you like, it will sift through all the masses of choices on offer and make your selection for you. (And if you ask it nicely, it might even fetch your slippers.)

Already here ... in a classroom near you!

Incredible e-ducation

In the good-old-bad-old days school kids used to be able to get up to all sorts of tricks to make their school lives easier. Such as...

a) Turning up at their secondary school, getting a register mark, then nicking off the lessons they didn't fancy going to. Or simply nicking off *all* of their lessons!

b) Telling their mum and dad they'd worked incredibly hard in class all day when they'd actually done nothing but daydream, lark about and chinwag with chums.

c) Telling mum and dad they'd got ace marks for last week's homework.

d) Accidentally on purpose losing their (horrendous) end of term report on the way home from school.

e) Telling mum and dad there was no homework tonight so it would be perfectly all right for them to go out with their mates (the kids' mates, not the parents').

The happiest days of your life ... ha ha

Forget it! Not any more they can't. By linking classrooms to living rooms the Incredible Internet is making sure that wheezes like those are things of the past.

Whenever they feel like it parents are now able to go online and immediately find out everything. With the new systems that are already up and running in some schools here's what they can do by a few clicks of the computer mouse:

a) Check the electronic register to make sure you're actually in school. And if you're at secondary school they can make sure you're attending *all* your lessons!

b) See what homework you've been set this week and have a butcher's at how you did with last week's homework.

c) See if there are any problems relating to your work and behaviour and find out what you and your teachers are doing to sort them.

d) Get a rolling report by taking a quick squizz at the results for all the tests you've done in class this week and looking at your teachers' comments about you.

e) See how you're matching up to the performance targets your teachers set you.

Don't do it! Big mother, brother (and almost every other) is watching!

And if that isn't bad enough they can actually watch you in class. All day long if they feel like it. Web cams positioned all around your classroom will make it possible for them to check on you whenever they feel like. Or spy on you all day long if they want to. Maybe in the company of a few friends. Those hated school tests could become the most popular spectator event in your street.

Of course there is one way you could turn all this online snooping to your advantage.

And finally, just to show you the future is much closer than you think, here are...

One: weather on toast

An inventor in Britain has designed a toaster that is linked to the local weather station by the Internet. When your bread is good 'n' golden a little template drops on to it, allowing the heating element to burn a symbol into your toast, telling you what the weather's likely to be today: a sun for fine weather, raindrops for wet weather and a cloud for overcast weather.

But, of course, this is nothing new or remarkable – fried eggs have been forecasting sunny days for centuries!

Two: Tele-graffiti

Thanks to the Incredible Internet you can now play noughts and crosses with your cousin Colin in Canada (or hangman with your Uncle Dave in Dartmoor) all without moving from your kitchen table! Here's what you do. You get a piece of  paper, scribble down your grid and bung in your first "X". As you do, a "Tele-graffiti" Internet camera and projector transmit your drawing via another Tele-graffiti set-up to a piece of paper on your cousin's kitchen table in Calgary, Canada. Your cousin then dobs in their "O" which immediately appears on your paper back in the UK. Well, to be honest, it doesn't appear immediately, there's actually a 70 millisecond delay. (Yes, very irritating … but you'll just have to learn to be patient.) Tele-graffiti isn't just for playing paper games with remote relatives and faraway friends. It can also be used for more serious purposes by people like architects, engineers (and bankrobbers), who can work on joint projects without having to fly halfway around the world to put their heads together.

Three: world wide whiffs

The main senses we use to receive information from the Internet are sight (to read text and look at pictures) and hearing (to listen to music and radio broadcasts). An Internet company in California decided that it would like to give web-heads the chance to surf 'n' sniff. The idea was to have a digital index of thousands and thousands of pongs: stench of swamp rat, fragrance of foxglove, odour of armpit … that sort of thing. Each smell would have its own file that would then be embedded in a website or an email. When you clicked on the email or the site the smells would come wafting out of a computer attachment at just the right moment, all blasted towards you by a little fan. The source of the smells would be a cartridge containing 28 basic smells that could be mixed to form an infinite variety of pongs in just the same way as the basic colours in an inkjet cartridge can be mixed to produce a vast range of colour shades. So when a farmyard full of windy cows appeared on your screen the smell-squirter would spring into action and kick out the appropriate pong. At the moment, development on this surf 'n' sniff project has come to a halt because the company working on it ran out of money, but no doubt someone who nose what they're doing will soon re-start the action.

WELL, YOU KNOW IT MAKES SCENTS!

STINK-O-TRON

Four: cyber-dolls

Do you remember how you used to set up your dollies and give them all names and personalities like stroppy Cindy and dozy Deborah, then treat them all to little tea parties. (Girls, maybe you did this too?) Well, readers, according to the futurologists (high-class fortune tellers) children in years to come won't have to go to all the trouble of exhausting their imaginations. They'll go online and download personalities, voices, memories and even personal tastes into their little plastic playmates. Then the dolls will yak to them, they'll yak to the dolls and the dolls will yak to each other. And before they know it they'll be plotting your overthrow.

Five: the Internet wardrobe

This one's for people who like to look the cat's whiskers rather than the dog's dinner but haven't got the time to be forever nipping down the shops and trying on the latest clobber. It's called the Internet wardrobe and it's a bit like the Internet fridge (but warmer). The wardrobe has built-in electronic sensors which read electronic tags on the clothes it contains, then "describes" their size, colour and style to the built-in computer. When you want a new teflon-lined cardigan to match your snazzy leather jogging flares the computer starts searching all the online clothes shops until it finds just the thing. Then, if you like it, you simply send some e-cash down the line and that's that.

LAST CLICKS

Digital deprivation – part two

Thousands of new pages are added to the World Wide Web each day. The Internet gets thousands of new users each week! Millions of emails are sent every hour! With so many people rushing to get hooked up it feels like everyone in the world will soon be online and enjoying the brilliant benefits of cyber-citizenship. Far from it! Just because the World Wide Web reaches all the way around the planet it doesn't necessarily mean that all of the planet's people are lucky enough to be able to reach the Incredible Internet.

Believe it or not!

- Despite its phenomenal popularity and growth only about 9% of the people in the world are connected to the Internet!

WELL, FOR A START THERE'S NOWHERE TO PLUG IT IN!

- In 2000 more than 80% of the people in the world had never even used a telephone ... never mind surfed the Web or sent an email! With the world population currently standing at about 6,000 million, that's about 4,800 million people altogether.

- One fifth of all the people in the world live in South Asia. Less than 1% of them have got a connection to the Internet.

- The Manhattan district of New York has more telephone lines than all the countries of Africa put together. On the continent of Africa there's only one phone line for every 53 people.

- Four-fifths of all websites are in English, a language understood by only one in 10 people on the planet.

And more to the point, while all the billions of poor people in the world haven't even got basic things like food, electricity, drinkable water, proper toilets, good health care, telephones and transport systems there doesn't seem to be much point in them surfing the Incredible Internet!

So, if you are online at home or have access to an Incredible Internet connection, count your blessings and make the most of it, perhaps by having a bash at the…

THE INCREDIBLE INTERNET TRIVIA CHALLENGE

Along with brilliant books, the Incredible Internet is a fact-fiend's friend, a knowledge-hound's nose and a trivia-tracker's dream. Prove the point and sharpen your surfing skills by tackling these quirky brain-benders. If you'd been asked these questions 15 years ago you'd have had to spend a month wandering around libraries, leafing through text books and interrogating experts in an attempt to find the solutions. But with the Incredible Internet the answers are just a few clicks away. Especially if you're a whizz with search engines! However, just in case you're a newbie, there are also some web addresses to give you a helping hand. OK! Time to...

Go get the knowledge!

1. During the year 1999 how many people in Britain were injured by...

a) trousers?

b) toilet roll holders?

c) tea cosies?

2. To the nearest second, how old will you be at 2.30 pm on 29th July 2032?

3. How long was the shortest war ever fought and where did it take place?

4. Which of the following famous people were cat haters and which ones were cat crazy?

a) Hitler

b) Charles Dickens

c) Napoleon

d) Florence Nightingale

e) Benito Mussolini

f) Genghis Khan

g) Winston Churchill

5. Why do sheep stare straight ahead of them when they're being chased?

AARGH! IT'S THE GIANT TEA COSY!

6. Convert 4,344,765 milligrams to pounds.

7. Could a frog survive after being swallowed by a cat then regurgitated?

8. What's your name in Japanese?

9. How tall will you be when you're 32?

10. Who invented the cat flap?

11. Why do most zips have the letters YKK on them? Oh come on … don't say you hadn't noticed!

12. What time does it get dark in London on 5th May?

13. Who are the tallest race of people in the world?

14. How many more people in the world are there than there were last Tuesday?

15. How do you escape from quicksand?

16. Name six famous people who were born on this day.

17. If a dog is seven years old how old is it in human years?

18. What's the Romanian word for pudding?

19. How many alligators have been found swimming in the sewers of New York?

20. At this moment what time is it in Hong Kong?

21. Why is sick green?

22. What *day* was the 23rd October 1929?

23. On average how many gallons of water does a human drink in a lifetime?

24. How far is it from Paris to Peking?

25. What colour is the national flag of Finland?

Here are the websites where you'll probably find the answers to the teasers. The clue might well be in the address.

www.didyouknow.com/fastfacts/bodyfastfacts.htm

phrases.shu.ac.uk/list/

cats.about.com/gi/dynamic/offsite.htm?site=http%3A%2F%2Fhome.att.net%2F%7Ek-doyle%2FCats%2Fcats4.htm

www.allaboutzanzibar.com/indepth/history/id-01-01-42-shortestwar.htm

www.newsandevents.utoronto.ca/bin2/thoughts/hand010625.asp

www.newscientist.com/lastword/answers/29top20.jsp?tp=top

www.nationalgeographic.com/features/97/nyunderground/docs/myth100.html

www.geocities.com/Athens/Parthenon/8107/convert.html

www.nationalgeographic.com/features/97/nyunderground/docs/myth100.html

www.census.gov/cgi-bin/ipc/popclockw

www.timeanddate.com/worldclock/

www.hhforcats.org/calculator/calculator.asp

www.knockdoctor.com/calculator/heightpredic.htm

www.theodora.com/flags/new/finland_flags.html

www.latin.org/english/name-lookup.html

www.geocities.com/Tokyo/Ginza/3379/japname.html

www.bowwow.com.au/calculator/index.asp

content.health.msn.com/heightpredict

www.users.globalnet.co.uk/~farley/abbey/lovers.html

209.130.72.188/nmerc/trivia_today.htm

www.thehistorynet.com/today/today.htm

www.expatpost.com/worlddistance/

www.xe.com/ucc/

www.worstcasescenarios.com/